THE HARVARD FIVE
IN NEW CANAAN

William D. Earls, AIA

THE HARVARD FIVE
IN NEW CANAAN

Midcentury Modern Houses by

MARCEL BREUER · LANDIS GORES · JOHN JOHANSEN · PHILIP JOHNSON · ELIOT NOYES & OTHERS

W. W. NORTON & COMPANY
NEW YORK · LONDON

For information about permission to reproduce selections from this book, write to Permissions,
W. W. Norton & Company, Inc., 500 Fifth Avenue, New York, NY 10110

Manufacturing by Quebecor World Kingsport Press
Book design and composition by Evil Empire
Production manager: Leeann Graham

Library of Congress Cataloging-in-Publication Data

Earls, William D.
     The Harvard Five in New Canaan : midcentury modern houses by Marcel Breuer,
     Landis Gores, John Johansen, Philip Johnson, Eliot Noyes & others / William D. Earls.-- 1st ed.
        p. cm.
Includes index.
ISBN-13: 978-0-393-73183-5 (hardcover)
ISBN-10: 0-393-73183-9 (hardcover)
1. Architecture, Domestic--Connecticut--New Canaan--History--20th century.
2. New Canaan (Conn.)--Buildings, structures, etc.
I. Title.
NA7238.N36E27 2006
728'.37097469--dc22

                                    2006007099

ISBN 13: 978-0-393-73183-5
ISBN 10: 0-393-73183-9

W. W. Norton & Company, Inc., 500 Fifth Avenue, New York, NY 10110
www.wwnorton.com

0 9 8 7 6 5 4 3 2 1

CONTENTS

1. DUNHAM 2. BREMER 3. GORES 4. BREUER 5. JOHANSEN 6. STACKPOLE 7. JOHNSON 8. HODGSON

MODERN HOUSE DAY

NEW CANAAN, CONNECTICUT

SUNDAY, MAY 25, 1952

This ticket admits one person to each of eight houses shown on map. Present at each home. $2.00.

1346

Mills House/Sherwood, Mills & Smith

INTRODUCTION

"What is a house? Most Americans, given this apparently easy question, would probably draw a picture—white clapboards, peaked shingled roof, red brick chimney, flagstone walk and green shutters—announce comfortably, "There. That's a house." But the residents of New Canaan, Connecticut, a 300-year-old Colonial village with an extremely high percentage of white clapboard and green-shutter houses, would not be so positive. They would be more likely to launch into an enthusiastic discussion of Mies van der Rohe, dropped girders, Thermopane glass and 'planned environment,' or into a disgusted denunciation of "cantilevered crackerboxes." Then they would take you out in a car and show you some of their houses. Because New Canaan, to its considerable surprise, has become an architects' battleground, and everyone talks houses."

HOLIDAY MAGAZINE, August 1952

Over fifty years ago, the "Harvard Five" architects, Marcel Breuer, Landis Gores, John Johansen, Philip Johnson, and Eliot Noyes, built houses for themselves and their clients in New Canaan, Connecticut.

What followed was a period when some of the best-known architects of the 20th century produced landmark designs in a community otherwise known for staunch New England conservatism. Set against a backdrop of old colonial houses and idyllic scenery, the modern houses incite strong reactions from nearly everyone who sees them, even today.

In 1949 the first modern house tour was held. Others soon followed, and the media of the day celebrated New Canaan as "the place to see in the East" for modern architecture. Even today, enthusiasts from around the world come to search out these icons found nestled in the countryside. A recent tour of six modern houses, with the proceeds to benefit a local charity, quickly sold out hundreds of tickets at $250 per person.

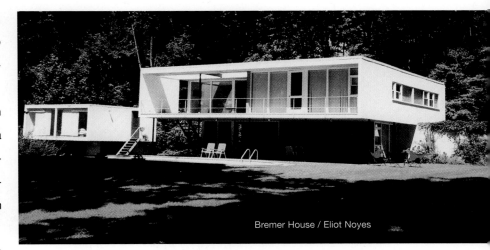

Bremer House / Eliot Noyes

In the 1950's, critics attacked the architects and their houses in humorous rhyming letters in the local newspaper, and the architects and their sympathizers responded in kind. These poems, collected for the first time, are included here in this book. Numerous excerpts from the media of that time have been included to give an indication of the excitement these houses generated.

Rayford House / Frank Lloyd Wright

New Canaan is a small town known for its many fine old houses, some dating back to the 1700's, on large wooded lots bordered by rambling stone walls. It is an affluent bedroom community within commuting distance of New York City, with a spur line of the Metro-North railroad ending in the middle of it's charming downtown. The cover of the local newspaper, the Advertiser, calls New Canaan "The Station Next to Heaven." The population of New Canaan in 1950 was about 8,000. Today it is over 19,000.

This book does not attempt to explore the theories behind the modern houses of New Canaan, but merely presents the houses in photographs and floor plans. Only the briefest obser-vations of the houses are included here. The analysis of any one of these houses could occupy an entire book, and it is my hope that the preliminary effort this book represents will lead to further investigation by others.

The houses have been arranged chronologically, with the earliest first. This list is not definitive; many houses have been omitted due to lack of available information. They have been identified by the year construction was completed, the last name of the first owner, and the architect. The architects Landis Gores and John Black Lee created lists of the modern houses some years ago, and these were relied upon for much of this information.

Precise addresses have been omitted to protect the occupants, since most of these houses are privately owned and not open to the public. Readers of this book are encouraged to respect the homeowners' privacy.

Line drawings of the floor plans for many of the houses were traced by the author from varied sources, and attempt to document the original floor plans without subsequent additions or alterations wherever possible. They are not shown in any particular scale and should be considered as artistic interpretations of the original architects intent.

Although many towns and cities across the United States have their fair share of modern houses, only New Canaan, and ironically because of its conservative personality, can claim to be the home of these five modern architects. This relatively brief period in history is now being lost forever as speculative builders replace small modern houses with new larger houses. Some of the houses shown here have already been demolished and this book may serve as their best surviving record.

The article that follows, New Canaan Modern: The Beginning 1947-1952, by Jean Ely, has been reprinted here as it first appeared in the New Canaan Historical Society Annual of 1967. I feel it is still the best account of that period even though it was written almost forty years ago. Although the article states that these young architects hungered for larger buildings to increase their reputations, they will probably be immortalized for their smaller projects. Marcel Breuer may best be remembered for the tubular steel chairs he designed while still in college. The typewriter Eliot Noyes designed for IBM is on permanent display at the Pompidou Center in Paris. Despite the many buildings Philip Johnson designed and all of the books written about his life, he will always be famous for the glass house he designed for himself in New Canaan.

Over a hundred modern houses probably dotted the landscape in New Canaan at one time, but no one will ever know for sure. Houses that seemed modern when they were built, such as some of the ranches, would not be counted as modern today. To make the count more difficult, there is no simple definition as to what exactly makes a house "modern."

For instance, not all modern houses have flat roofs. The Smallen house and the Kniffen house have steeply pitched roofs. The Gores house and Irwin pool house have long, low-pitched roofs with deep overhangs.

Some, like the Parsons house and the first Lee house, are delicate white boxes with great expanses of glass. Others, such as the second house Noyes built for his own family, use the local fieldstone to create massive, windowless stone facades that face the street.

The house Philip Johnson built for himself sits as a pristine object on a manicured lawn, while the McCarthy house by Gelbin is clad in wood shingles and is nestled in the woods.

The Ball house by Johnson is an example of a typical modern

Rayford House / Frank Lloyd Wright

house without surface decoration or ornament. By contrast, the Warner house by Johansen has salmon colored stucco exterior walls with constellation designs etched into its surface.

Many of these houses were built on modest budgets. John Black Lee recalls using a ping-pong table as part of the building materials of one of the houses. Conversely, the Day house he designed used luxurious materials that indicate that budget was not always a primary constraint.

The floor plans of many of these houses are not characteristically modern either. Although modern architecture is known for balanced, asymmetrical plans, such as the Stackpole house by Noyes, many of these houses have rigid, symmetrical floor plans, such as the Dunham house by Johansen and several houses by John Black Lee. The strict symmetry of these houses is in direct contrast to what they were taught as students of modern architecture by Gropius, their mentor at Harvard.

So if there is no one characteristic that makes these houses modern, or if there is no particular "New Canaan Modern" style, what is it that these houses have in common? I don't believe these architects or their clients were interested in following any prescribed path. They simply wanted that indescribable feeling of living in a modern house.

The Harvard Five architects were relatively wealthy young men. Although these individuals may have enjoyed special advantages, they must still be given credit for taking chances with their careers and reputations. The house Eliot Noyes built for himself in 1947 was the first truly modern house in New Canaan. The second house he built required that he and his family walk outdoors to pass from bedrooms to living room. He used his own houses as experiments, with little regard for conventional public opinion.

The first house Marcel Breuer built for himself pushed the limits of wood construction in the pursuit of the defeat of gravity. Philip Johnson, although already very wealthy before he graduated architecture school, did not lead a life of idle luxury, but instead pursued design commissions and worked well into his nineties. John Johansen continues to stretch the envelope of architectural theory, building models and writing books about architecture.

Some critics denounce the Harvard Five as part of a small, liberal group that could not have been in tune with the majority of conservative New Canaanites. However, these architects were hired to design large buildings, including skyscrapers, embassies and colleges. They had ties to an echelon of conservative business clientele that any architect would envy.

It may be ironic to regard modern houses as historically significant, since the houses themselves appear to have a disregard for history. The modern architects insisted they had a deep respect for the past, drawing upon the underlying lessons of history. They were attempting to build according to the best technology of the age, embracing innovation in the same manner as the architects of the ancient gothic cathedrals.

Modern houses are occasionally still built in New Canaan. But most of the architects who design these houses live elsewhere. That is probably what makes this story unique; that these architects ever lived and found clients in the small, conservative New England town of New Canaan in the first place.

Some say a similar phenomenon will never happen again. Of course it couldn't happen in exactly the same way. But those who say it couldn't happen again are just the kind who would have never seen it coming in the first place.

NEW CANAAN MODERN: THE BEGINNING 1947–1952

by JEAN ELY

Reprinted with permission of the author and The New Canaan Historical Society.

First published in The New Canaan Historical Society Annual–1967

Twenty years ago New Canaan architecture meant the clapboard house, pitched roof, and balanced composition of the colonial idiom. This was architecture of the past—an architecture that for over two hundred years was comfortable, harmonious, traditional, familiar. These houses have become history. They remain as genuine expressions of their time. But architecture has changed.

Since the late 1940s New Canaan has come to be known for a new kind of architecture—a modern architecture outside of the tradition of colonialism and the past. The modern movement—with its experimentation in material, construction methods, space, and form—is architecture of the present. Like the clapboard colonial, the modern house is built as an expression of its time. The colonial clapboard is today's history. The modern house is the history of tomorrow.

AMERICAN MODERN: THE ORIGINS

The modern movement in architecture–the change from a traditional to a contemporary idiom, came about gradually in this country during the late 1800s and early 1900s through a combination of native American thought and design with European thought and design. The American antecedents of the modern movement can be seen in the work of such giants as: H. H. Richardson, Louis Sullivan, Stanford White, Frank

Wiley House / Philip Johnson

Lloyd Wright. It finds its greatest expression in the skyscrapers of the Chicago School and the "Prairie Houses" of Wright.

In Europe the modern movement found a focal point in the German Bauhaus—a loose union of free thinking artists and craftsman led by Walter Gropius—that from 1919 to 1933 strove to unite art and industrial life and to find a basis for a sound contemporary architecture. The Bauhaus was a school, a philosophy, an ideal, an approach to teaching and design. First in Weimar, Germany, later in Dessau, these creative revolutionaries worked, taught, and experimented in all the art forms, giving vent to new expressions in theater, dance, art, industrial design, and architecture. Its teachers, or "form masters" numbered among the great artists and designers of this century: Paul Klee, Lyonel Feininger, Josef Albers, Marcel Breuer, Laszlo Moholy-Nagy, Wassily Kandinsky. And when in

McCarthy House / Allen Gelbin

six men were products of the Harvard Graduate School of Design and Gropius's revolutionary teaching. Marcel Breuer, Eliot Noyes, John Johansen, Landis Gores, Philip Johnson, and Victor Christ-Janer constituted New Canaan modern. They were the first wave.*

THE HARVARD FIVE

Marcel Breuer, born in Hungary in 1902, was the eldest of this group and having studied (1920–1924 at the Bauhaus in Weimer) and taught (1924–1928 at the Dessau Bauhaus) was obviously the most directly influenced by Gropius and the Bauhaus orientation. From 1937 to 1946 he taught architecture and design at Harvard, practiced architecture with Gropius, and became a prime mover in the modern movement.

During these years, the late 1930s and early 1940s, the teaching of architecture in this country was completely revolutionized. The old academic standards were suddenly unacceptable and out of date. At Harvard the old Beaux-Arts faculty was thrown over to make way for the new movement. The generation of architects graduating was the first to be trained completely in the modern idiom. They were "in the front" and they knew it.

Eliot Noyes, born in Boston in 1910, was the first of this generation of New Canaan modern architects to emerge, graduating from Harvard in 1938 with a Masters degree in architecture. Yet but for a skill in watercoloring, Noyes might not have figured among the Gropius-Breuer trained group. From 1935 to

1933 political pressure in Germany began to make creative expression impossible, the Bauhaus disbanded—letting loose its students, teachers, ideas and ideals upon the world.

The founder and chief proponent of the Bauhaus, Walter Gropius, first went to London. Then in 1937 he came to this country to teach at Harvard's Graduate School of Design, bringing with him his one time pupil and colleague, architectural partner and friend, Marcel Breuer. Together they signaled the beginning of a new wave of thought and design, a new method of teaching, a new freedom of expression. In 1937 modernism took its chair at Harvard.

And ten years later put its foot in New Canaan. The year 1947 marks the beginning of the modern movement in New Canaan. In the following five years from 1947 to 1952 the town became the showcase of six modern architects. Five of these

* New Canaan's well known Willis N. Mills, whose architectural training (B. Arch. University of Pennsylvania 1929) preceded the real advent of modernism in this country falls somewhat outside this category, and for this reason his work is not included in this article.

1937, in the midst of his design training, Noyes left Cambridge to join in an archaeological expedition to Persepolis in Persia. The Harvard that Noyes came back to was a far different one than the one he had left. The tempo and emphasis of the conservative Cambridge training had changed with the arrival of Gropius and Breuer. But Noyes's interest in architecture began many years before the Bauhaus masters arrived on the scene. In undergraduate days, Noyes had found himself listening to a young Ohioan, Philip Johnson, who expounded freely on the merits of modern architecture and the lack of good architectural design at Harvard. At a time when most professors at Harvard were calling the new movement "shoebox design," Johnson was foresighted indeed. In 1938 Noyes left graduate school completely won over to this new movement in design and joined the staff at Gropius's and Breuer's office in Cambridge. The following year at Gropius' instigation, Noyes accepted an appointment as Director of the Department of Industrial Design at New York City's Museum of Modern Art, a position he held both before and after the war. Though trained for architecture, Noyes, then as later, felt no difficulty in working with industrial design. It can only be a coincidence that Noyes went to the museum where his old school friend, Philip Johnson, headed the Department of Architecture and Design.

John Johansen (born 1916 in New York) was the next New Canaan architect to come out of Harvard. Studying architecture as an undergraduate and graduate, Johansen when he received his B. Arch. in 1941 was perhaps the most thoroughly indoctrinated, educated in the Gropius–Breuer framework of thought and design. Like Noyes, Johansen worked at the office of Gropius and Breuer before starting out on his own. And as Noyes had done and Breuer was later to do, Johansen came to New York where he worked in the architectural firm of Skid-

more, Owings & Merrill until setting up his own practice in 1948.

Following in the Harvard Graduate School line was Landis Gores (born 1919 in Ohio), who graduated in 1942, four years behind Noyes, a year behind Johansen, and a year ahead of Johnson. Unlike the other Harvard graduates, Gores and his close friend and fellow Ohioan, Johnson, were mavericks. Johnson, who had studied Greek and history of architecture at Harvard, and Gores, who had focused on Greek and English at Princeton, were not as susceptible to the Bauhaus–Cambridge line as Noyes and Johansen. The two "bad-boys," Gores recalled, "had a certain feeling of community, a common outlook." Gores found the architecture of Frank Lloyd Wright more to his liking, while Johnson leaned toward the classic simplicity of Mies van der Rohe, another arrival from the Bauhaus. And yet Gropius was to both men "a great figure to whom we all owe a lot."

Philip Johnson (born 1906 in Ohio) had graduated from Harvard with a B.A. in 1927, a full ten years before Gropius and Breuer emigrated and long before the others began to think

McCarthy House / Allen Gelbin

Johnson House / Philip Johnson

about architecture. After leaving college, Johnson divided his time between touring abroad and setting up a new department at the Museum of Modern Art in New York, the Department of Architecture and Design—the first of its kind in this country. Johnson ran this department from its beginning in 1932 until 1954, initiating exhibitions of the modern movement, exposing the American public to its first taste of the "International Style." In his travels, Johnson saw the significance and meaning of the new architecture of Europe. His taste inclined toward the elegant statements of Mies van der Rohe, the young German who headed the Bauhaus from 1930 to 1933 after Gropius's resignation in 1928. In 1940, thirteen years after leaving Harvard, Philip

Johnson returned to enter the Graduate School of Design, graduating three years later.

THE WAR AND AFTER

World War II split apart the Cambridge group of Breuer, Noyes, Johansen, Gores, and Johnson. People went into the service and lost contact with each other. Life was disrupted. And in a country whose energies were devoted to winning a war fought on foreign shores, there was little time for budding architects. But projects were started and designs were made for the day when the world would turn to architecture instead of arms. A post–world war environment required a different type of architecture—an architecture of simplicity and meaning—an architecture the Gropius trained group was fully qualified and eager to provide.

After the war, Johansen recalled, "We were all glad to find each other again and talk." New York became the gathering place. By 1946 Breuer, Noyes, Johansen, Gores, and Johnson had come to the city to work, to put to use all that they had stored up at Harvard, all that the war had disrupted. In that year Breuer left his teaching position at Harvard and the architectural office he shared with Gropius in Cambridge and settled down to practice in New York. His student Eliot Noyes in the meantime had left the Air Force and his position at the Museum of Modern Art and, wanting "to get back into the world of doing things," had gone to work at the office of Norman Bel Geddes, leading New York industrial designer. Johansen found himself working at Skidmore, Owings & Merrill. And Gores and Johnson, independents that they were, had set up shop on their own.

Among this group of five, cross currents and communication were natural and inevitable. All had the Cambridge–Gropius heritage. Johnson and Noyes had both worked at the Museum of Modern Art and had exhibited the work of their teacher and friend, Marcel Breuer. Noyes and Johansen had both done apprentice work with Gropius and Breuer in Cambridge. And Johnson and Gores, the two Ohioans, stuck together naturally and worked on projects together.

While the Cambridge five were all busy over their drafting boards in New York, the last actor in the drama of New Canaan modernism, Victor Christ-Janer (born 1915 in Minnesota) was just finishing his architectural training at Yale.

Two years later in 1949 the six architects found themselves buying land, designing and building houses, living miles outside of New York City in the town of New Canaan, Connecticut.

NEW CANAAN: THE FOCUS

The move to New Canaan started with Eliot Noyes who felt the itch to practice on his own and in 1947 left the office of Bel Geddes with a plum in his pocket—the IBM typewriter account. Years before, while working on the air force glider program, Noyes had met Thomas J. Watson, Jr. and had spent some pleasant weekends catching air currents over Virginia with the IBM executive. When Noyes decided to work independently, the IBM account was his, complete with a $400 monthly retainer for his efforts. Soon after leaving Bel Geddes, Noyes decided to move his family out to Westport, Connecticut. In post-war New York decent apartment space for a growing family just was not to be had. Noyes liked Westport and made an offer on some land but was turned down. The real estate broker mentioned nearby New Canaan as a likely possibility and the Noyeses made an appointment to inspect a site there. "It was raining like hell the night before and we said if it isn't a good day tomorrow, the hell with New Canaan." Tomorrow came and the sun shone and the Noyeses bought the property. Noyes finished building his house, moved his family in, set up office in town, and stayed there.

The first Noyes house located on Lambert Road was an unusual sight for the traditionally oriented town. Noyes recalled that when the model for his proposed house was finished he was afraid to show it around. "There were no modern houses here then."

The town suited Noyes. He liked its proximity to New York, the availability of land, its compact size, its organization, its zoning. And knowing a good thing, he told his friends about it. At the time Johnson and Breuer were both looking in the Stamford area for land to build on. Noyes told Johnson about his own luck in New Canaan and put his friend in touch with a broker, who showed the architect a five-acre site on Ponus Ridge. Johnson bought the property and built his Glass House there two years later in 1949. Breuer, encouraged by Noyes, had bought land on Sunset Hill Road, and built his cantilevered residence there in 1947. Unlike the other four architects in town, Johnson and

town itself was pleasing and as Breuer put it, "I liked the commute. It was just the right amount of time traveling if you had to take the train (the New Haven was better organized in those days) and if you had to drive it was possible to keep the sun behind one's back in the morning going in and in the evening going out." Johnson had other reasons for coming out to the country: "I came here because Breuer and Noyes were here and I wanted to be in a community of architects and the laws here in Connecticut regarding licensing were not as strict as in New York."

Day House / John Black Lee

When Gores and Johnson had so independently set up their practice in New York after the war, they did so without regard to licensing. Neither was a registered architect in the state. In those days the New York license required that a young architect be apprenticed to a registered architect for three years to qualify for the registration exams. Neither Gores nor Johnson wanted to go

Breuer kept their offices and apartments in New York, using their New Canaan homes as weekend and summer retreats —for Breuer as a place to bring up his son and relax with friends, for Johnson as bachelor's quarters and release from the pace of the city.

Noyes admitted, "We wanted our pals around." The

through the ordeal of an apprenticeship and found Connecticut, where an apprenticeship was not required, more to their liking. In 1948, the year after Noyes, Breuer, and Johnson bought land in New Canaan, Landis Gores took the Connecticut exams and became licensed. Johnson, who did not take the exams in Connecticut until later, continued to work with Gores until 1951, when Gores set up his own practice and Johnson returned to New York to make his peace with the powers that be.

Of the early modern houses the house that Johnson built was the hardest for the town to understand. Three years in design, two years in construction, the now classic Glass House then seemed scandalous, indecent, shocking to the town. The house, a house without walls, without rooms, built of glass was an architectural revolution in itself. This particular house, "the most publicized house in the United States," has come to define and stand for the modern movement in general.

Landis Gores, Johnson's close friend and partner, was the fourth member of the group to move to New Canaan. He and his wife, seeking the space and luxury of the country, found four acres of land on Cross Ridge Road in 1947 and built their house there the following year. Their house, a horizontal modulation of Wrightian massing, in contrast to Johnson's Glass House, was the easiest for the town traditionalists to live with. It was, as one New Canaanite put it, "a modern house that looked like a house."

The one Yale-trained architect to arrive on the scene, Victor Christ-Janer, came in 1949 due to the mishaps of a faulty generator and a wandering cat. Tired of New York, the Christ-Janers had gone one weekend to visit in-laws in New Haven. On the way home a failing generator made them turn off the Merritt Parkway at the New Canaan exit to find a garage. "Our cat got out of the car and went romancing. It was raining and after the generator was fixed we sat in the car and waited for the cat to come back. We sat there in the garage lot all night. I knew none of these architects. I didn't even know they were here. The morning was sunny when the

Teaze House / John Black Lee.

cat showed up. We took a wrong turn on our way back to the parkway. We passed a field on Frogtown Road and my wife said 'That's where I want to live'. We came back a week later and bought it."

That same year, John Johansen arrived in town and as Noyes and Gores had done set up practice on his own. Like Breuer and Johnson, Johansen's first contact with New Canaan came about through a visit to his friend Eliot Noyes. "It was a convenient town, far enough but not too far from New York. It was well organized." Following the direction of Johnson's good fortune, Johansen found land on Ponus, buying nine or ten acres to get the five he wanted. "You could get a chunk then big enough to do what you wanted and to have privacy at the same time." By 1951 Johansen had finished his house.

With the exception of Breuer, those architects were all just getting started. They welcomed each other's presence. It was, as Johnson remembered, "a close group, a neat group."

Warner House / John Johansen

abroad, if they knew one, saw all."

In the spring of 1949 New Canaan had its first formally organized modern house tour, with the houses of Eliot Noyes (chairman of this first tour), Landis Gores, Philip Johnson, Marcel Breuer, Ogden Kniffen (designed by Noyes and Breuer), Talbot Rantoul, and Edward E. Mills on view. The tour, fully and glowingly reviewed by the *New Canaan Advertiser*, the *New York Times*, and various professional journals, brought over a thousand interested and curious people into these seven modern houses built since the war. It also brought some $2,000 into the coffers of the New Canaan Library Building Fund. People came and saw. The houses conquered. By 1953, four years later, the seven modern houses had multiplied in number four times over.

They built their homes as much to exhibit their learning and design ideas as to put a roof over their heads. They felt unique, and they were. The group met often at each other's houses to air opinions, share problems, discuss ideas. To them New Canaan became a watering hole, a gathering place for their friends out from New York, down from Cambridge, or over from Europe. Gores remembered the camaraderie of the early days: "We had the time then. In the old days we were all in and out of each others' houses. Visitors and friends from this country and

Johansen recalled, "The five or six architects that gathered here served an almost educational aspect, teaching as well as designing the modern." The word spread and soon the architects found clients, people willing to break out of the traditional mold into the freedom and expression of the modern. Noyes and Breuer in a brief and informal partnership in 1948 finished the Kniffen house on Turtleback Road. Noyes himself who seemed the busiest in the early days, also had to his credit three houses on Ponus Ridge—the Moseley house (1948), the Talman house (1949), the Stackpole house (1951) plus the Bremer house on Weed Street (1952), the Ault house on Lambert (1952) and the Weeks house on Valley Road (1952). In 1951 Gores and Johnson finished the Richard Hodgson house across from Johnson's own home. Johansen, last of the group to finish his own house in 1951, was hard at work on the Hobbs-Durham house on Woods End Road and the Campbell house on Laurel Road. In 1952 Victor Christ-Janer worked on the Roles house on Wahackme and the Gratwick-Simonsen house on Myanos. Breuer and Noyes, whose first houses were modest in cost and material, went on to design second homes for themselves. Breuer's fieldstone and glass house on West Road was finished in 1951; Noyes's elegant Country Club Road house was completed three years later.

By 1952 New Canaan, as Johnson put it, "had become the place to see in the East." Though the modern houses numbered only thirty at that time, thousands of people came to see them. Students and critics of architecture studied them and the reaction of the professional world of art and design was one of great admiration and appreciation.

THE TOWN REACTS

The reaction in the town itself was not so wholeheartedly approving. In March 1952 the issue came to a head. Johnson's then controversial Glass House seemed to be the most criticized and ridiculed by the town traditionalists. The house attracted huge weekend crowds, caused traffic jams on Ponus, and necessitated policemen in the area to keep order. Many felt the house more a detriment than an asset to the community. The flat-roofed boxes were, as the conservatives saw it,

ruining the countryside, marring the beauty of nearby traditional New England architecture. Johnson, like the other architects, heard the criticism but continued to work, to open his house for inspection, to speak to local citizens.

On March 6, 1952 Johnson gave a talk to the local Kiwanis Club, explaining the modernism of the new houses and architects in town. A week later the Readers Views section of the *New Canaan Advertiser* printed the following poem by "Ogden Gnash Teeth," pseudonym of investment counselor Lewis Mack:

> *I see by the Advertiser of March 6, Page 7, Column 4*
> *That Mr. Philip (Glass House) Johnson,*
> > *with modesty galore,*
> *Lets the Kiwanis in on the secret that New Canaan*
> > *has become world famous*
> *(He should have said notorious) because he and*
> > *Eliot Noyes and Walter Gropius*
> *And Landis Gores and John Johansen and*
> *Marcel Breuer and probably more as equally obnoxious*
> *Have graciously condescended to settle here*
> > *and ruin the countryside with packing boxes*
> *And partially opened bureau drawers set on steel*
> > *posts and stanchions …*
> *An architectural form as gracious as Sunoco*
> > *service stations.*

Not unpredictably the poem set off a barrage of poems that fed the feud between the traditionalists and modernists in New Canaan for the following five weeks. The poems, mostly unsympathetic to the modern movement, ranged from the amusing to the ridiculous. In self-defense the architects sent in their own effort under Landis Gores's name:

We see by the Advertiser of March 13, Page 4, Column 6,
That in the craw of Mr. Gnash Teeth modern
    architecture sticks,
Allergic to glass, steel, bureau drawers,
    and cantilevers,
A stuffy old stuffed-shirt with green myopic fever
Undulant, ruminant, tobacco on his vest,
Grandiloquent grandson of a grandson of the best,
Who latterly has failed, we fear to grasp in the slightest
That that which was found good in the past is no
    longer today the object of affection of
    the brightest–
That pigeons chalk his widows' walk, while widows
    chauffeur-driven
In sportscars pop from soda to lingerie shop, in the
    Station Next to Heaven.

In mid-April, perhaps with the coming of spring and warm weather, the feud ended almost as abruptly as it had begun. And the second modern house tour took place as scheduled in May, including the Bremer and Stackpole houses by Noyes, the Dunham house by Johansen, the Hodgson house by Johnson and Gores, the second Breuer house, Gores house, Johansen house, and Johnson house on display. Despite a heavy rain all day, 1,100 people attended bringing in some $2,200 to the community nursery school.

By 1952 the six architects—ridiculed by a few vocal towns-people, visited by the thousands attending the biannual house tours, and hired by a growing number of progressive residents —were firmly established—at least in the residential market. But they wanted more. Like any architect today, these six New Canaan architects knew that the reality of architecture lay in the institutional building—the schools, hospitals, libraries and theaters that affected the public on a much broader scale than the private residence. All sought institutional work. When during the summer of 1952 the design of a new school came up, the local architects, tired of seeing job after job go to out of town and occasionally lesser talent, banded together into a mutual aid society. In August Fairfield Associated Architects, with offices at 89 Main Street, submitted their joint services and talents to the town for the design of the new high school. The group, composed of Landis Gores, John Johansen, Victor Christ-Janer, Philip Johnson, Severin Stockmar, and landscape architect James Fanning, hoped that the design committee would be won over by such a collection of talented local architects. It wasn't. Eliot Noyes, though not a member of the short-lived Fairfield Associated Architects, was also hopeful of getting the commission and put in his bid separately. But he too was disappointed. The job went out of town.

Even later these architects were ignored for the large-scale civic jobs in town. Noyes, who in the sixties felt this may be for the best, did not want to get in the position of fighting the town for design: "I've lived and practiced here for twenty years and still can't get any big work here. If the town wanted to be an example of civic architecture, then I'd want to be a part of it very much."

By the late 1960s four of the six original architects still lived in their first homes, four continued to maintain offices in town, four had more work outside of the state than within. All were successful. All were discouraged. But they hade lost the illusions and dreams of young architects. Johnson felt that the New Canaan modern movement was really history. "Nothing is really happening now". One feels they weare disenchanted with the town. Johansen said, "New Canaan is like a wife you have

Gate House / Philip Johnson

been married to for twenty years. She's comfortable, familiar. You know where everything is. But the romance is gone." Yet all admitted they could never move. They echoed Johnson's words: "I would never move or build another house. This house is me, you see."

SUMMING UP

By the end of 1952 there were more than thirty modern houses in the town of New Canaan, most of them designed by the original group of Noyes, Breuer, Johnson, Gores, Johansen, and Christ-Janer. The reaction of the town to this phenomenon was, as one looks back on it, understandable. This was an architecture that burst on the scene. And like the uninvited guest, many a resident wished for some forewarning. But the initial reaction of outrage and anger changed gradually over the years to acceptance and pride. Until many could now agree with Victor Christ-Janer:

"After all, colonial and modern architecture aren't so very different in essence. Both styles grow from integrity in the use of materials and construction methods. Both are innovations. The colonials gave the Europeans an awful shock by using wood instead of stone. 'Salt Box' was once a derogatory term, you know. Both periods use the central fireplace and both are conscious of the importance of the outdoors which surrounds the house. Probably our ancestors would have had glass walls too, but they couldn't get panes any larger than six by eight inches. The main difference is in our culture and our different philosophy of space and proportions."

Intersection of South Avenue and Elm street, New Canaan

HOUSE TOUR

Eliot Noyes outside his first house in New Canaan

NOYES HOUSE 1
ELIOT NOYES ARCHITECT
1947

Eliot Noyes

The street level contained the bedrooms and entry foyer. Living room, dining room, kitchen, and study were located on the lower level, giving privacy from the street, direct access to the backyard, and views to the pond below.

The house has been demolished.

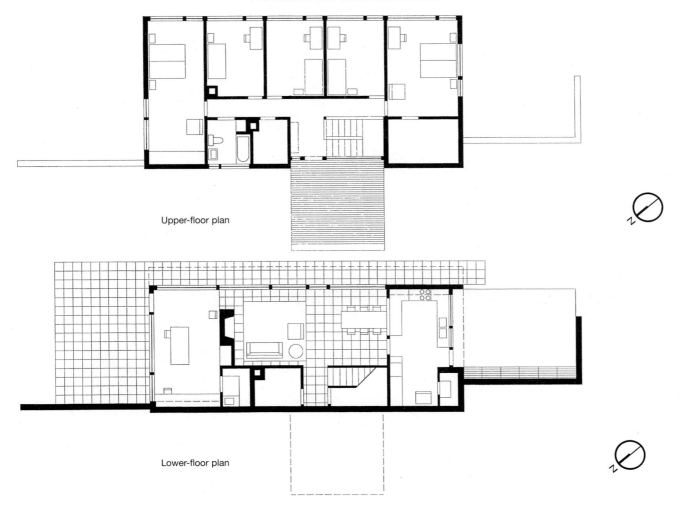

Upper-floor plan

Lower-floor plan

Entry

House from the southwest side

"As every reader of this magazine knows, New Canaan is the home of men like Marcel Breuer, Philip Johnson, Eliot Noyes, John Johansen, Landis Gores and others. They have made New Canaan a symbol of creativeness in modern American architecture."

HOUSE & HOME, January 1953

View from end of driveway

Landis Gores

GORES HOUSE
LANDIS GORES ARCHITECT *1948*

This exceptionally large modern house, now listed on the National Register of Historic Places, is based on the Prairie Style, but the detailing is influenced by the International Style. The doors and windows are exceptionally tall and detailed with machine-like quality. A massive overhang at the front door hovers surprisingly low, adding human scale even before one enters. The entry procession winds around the back of a stone fireplace, and only then does the grand living room express its full height. This main living space has so much glass that artificial light is not needed even on an overcast New England day.

Approach to house

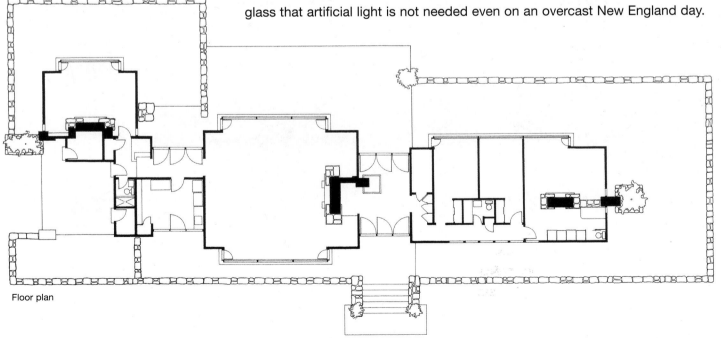
Floor plan

Entry

"Mrs. Gores said she didn't get a lot of input into the design of the house other than a steel frame in the ceiling of the main section of the house so a helicopter could land on the roof her long-time dream (not yet realized) and a blue bath tub in the master bedroom."

HOUSE & HOME, January 1952

Roof overhang detail

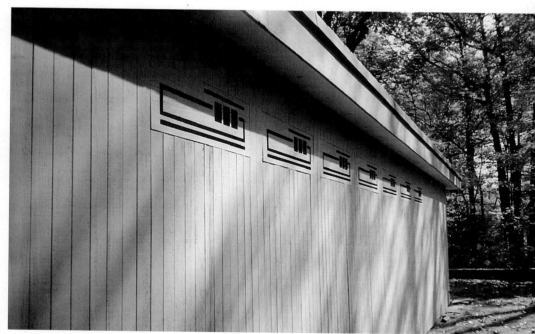

Detail in wall to right of front door

"Not only the tall living room, the entrance lobby and the stone ramparts on the valley side of the house proclaim its almost aristocratic scale; there is an almost aristocratic grace about the way of life which the house implies. Landis Gores is a creative young conservative among his avant-garde contemporaries. There are many like him in modern American literature, poetry and philosophy, but in architecture his work is still an isolated phenomenon."

HOUSE & HOME, January 1952

View from inside foyer through back door

Living room

Built-in furniture in dining area

Back of house

"It is modern because its plan is open and its spaces dynamic and bold; because its details are clean and simple; because it is intimately related to the landscape surrounding it; and because its many flat roofs and its large sheets of glass are the technology of our time.

"It is traditional because it was consciously designed in the living tradition of American domestic architecture, picking up this tradition at about the point of Frank Lloyd Wright's 1912 Coonley Playhouse; because its composition is almost symmetrical, both in the whole and in many of its parts; because its scale is monumental and its composition is three-dimensional; and because it is a deliberate attempt to emphasize the permanence of "home" rather than the temporariness of "industrialized shelter."
HOUSE & HOME, January 1952

View from street

"Is there today such a thing as a demonstrative architectural form? Is there a structural symbol comparable to the archaic column, the Gothic arch, the Renaissance dome? It is, perhaps, the cantilevered slab–light and slightly resilient in the wind …."

MARCEL BREUER

Marcel Breuer

BREUER HOUSE 1
MARCEL BREUER ARCHITECT *1948*

"New Canaan (pop. 8001) is a conservative, pretty, station-wagon town in handsome Fairfield County, within fashionable commuting distance of New York. Its startling notoriety began some six years ago when Marcel Breuer, one of the world's best-known and most admired contemporary architects, moved in and built himself a small but dramatic house, a long, one-story building suspended in mid-air over a platform by means of cantilevering and steel cables. Breuer is a master, and masters, of course, attract disciples. In no time at all New Canaan had a colony of new, T-square-carrying residents all busily designing new houses for themselves."

HOLIDAY, August 1952

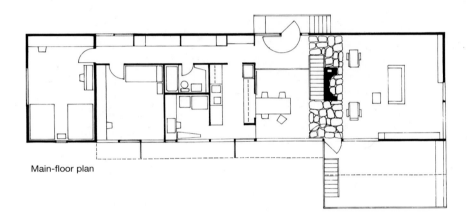

Main-floor plan

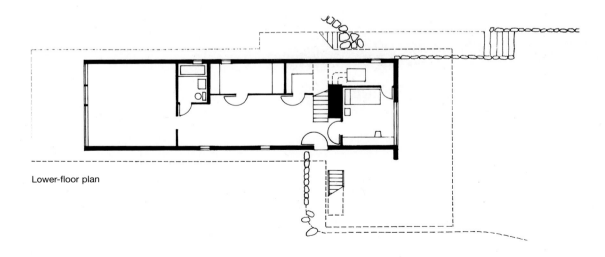

Lower-floor plan

37

Front of house

"Until recently, the only way to build was to exploit the dead weight of stones or bricks or wooden logs, to pile one on top of the other; beams or arches that depended upon gravity or compression-principle for their strength. The great change in construction has been the shift from simple compression structures to continuous, fluent tension-structures. This change is so radical that it alone would justify a completely new architectural concept. The past used gravity to defeat gravity; the Egyptian pyramid is broad at the base and narrowing to a point at the top. The "new structure" in its most expressive form is hollow below and substantial on top—just the reverse of the pyramid. It represents a new epoch in the history of man, the realization of one of his oldest ambitions; the defeat of gravity...."

MARCEL BREUER

"Somebody said 'architecture is frozen music.' This is true, though I have my reservations about the word 'frozen.' How about opening the doors, sliding open the windows or walls, going in and out, moving the chairs? How about the curtains, the changing light, color, and atmosphere…you not only see or photograph architecture, you live in it. It should be alive, not 'frozen.'

"Somebody else said it's a 'machine for living.' Again true, but you don't want to get greasy if you lean against the wall. You want to have something simpler, more elemental, more generous, and more human than a machine."

MARCEL BREUER

Marcel Breuer in his first house

Side of house

"As a result, we can now cantilever structures way out into the air—either horizontally, or vertically, as in a skyscraper. In either case, the seemingly unsupported structure reaching out into air is really tied to the rest of the building and to the ground. The whole skeleton of the building is a continuously integrated frame, and any stress on one part of it is resisted by all other parts of the frame. It is the principle of the tree: a structure cantilevered out of the ground, with branches and twigs in turn cantilevered out from the central tree trunk...."

MARCEL BREUER

Marcel and Constance Breuer on the cantilevered deck

"The real impact of any work is the extent to which it unifies contrasting notions, opposing points of view. The easy method of meeting contrasting problems is the feeble compromise. The solution for the contrasts between black and white is gray— that is the easy way. Sun and shadow does not mean a cloudy day."

MARCEL BREUER

Front of house

JOHNSON HOUSE
PHILIP JOHNSON ARCHITECT
1949

Philip Johnson

Innumerable books and magazine articles have been written about the Glass House. The entire estate, encompassing a collection of buildings, is often simply referred to as the Glass House. Philip Johnson left this property to the National Trust for Historic Preservation.

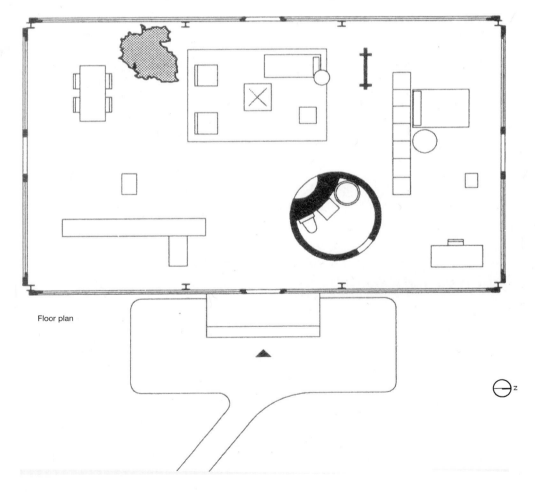

Floor plan

"Week-end crowds have been blocking traffic on Ponus Ridge in this conservative old community of early colonial homes, with hundreds of residents turning out in holiday mood to inspect Philip C. Johnson's all glass house. While workmen put the finishing touches on the 'private' residence and the adjoining guest house, startled, uninvited visitors tramp about to view the results with mingled expressions of awe, wonder and indignation. They agree that nothing like it ever was seen in these parts."

THE NEW YORK TIMES,
December 1948

Guest house, pool, and Glass House

"It was the first piece of property shown to me, five acres of tall, dense scrub and large trees sloping down from an old stone wall on the road. There was an open, flat area on a bluff looking west with a grand view of the Rippowam Valley. I liked it immediately and didn't look any further."

PHILIP JOHNSON

SCULPTURE GALLERY (1970)

PAINTING GALLERY (1965)

POOL (1955)

GLASS HOUSE (1949)

GUEST HOUSE (1949)

PAVILION AT POND (1962)

LINCOLN KIRSTEIN TOWER (1985)

Ponus Ridge Road

GATE (1981)

GATE HOUSE (1995)

LIBRARY STUDY (1980)

GHOST HOUSE (1984)

0'   150'   300'   600'

Site plan

Guest house interior

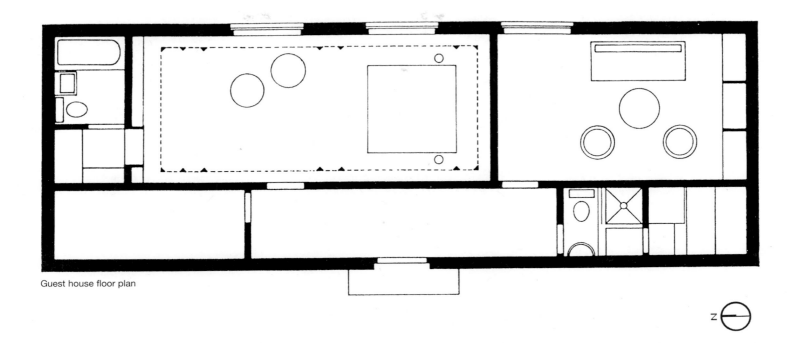

Guest house floor plan

N

Located on a diagonal path across from the Glass House, the Guest House is the "solid" to contrast with the "void" of the Glass House. Three large round windows are placed along the back, with only a blank door facing the Glass House.

View from Glass House to entry of guest house

Painting gallery interior

The painting gallery is almost completely buried, with only the cylindrical profile of its' plan visible from the street. The idea of a buried painting gallery was to preserve the art from damaging sunlight. To avoid what Philip Johnson called "museum fatigue," the gallery is purposefully small and requires no walking around to view the artwork. The paintings are hung on walls that can be manually rotated on huge spindles.

Entry to painting gallery

Painting gallery plan

N

Sculpture gallery interior

The sculpture gallery is also a windowless building, but its roof is entirely of steel and glass. The floor drops through a series of steps and levels. The white painted brick walls and numerous levels are remindful of a Greek island town.

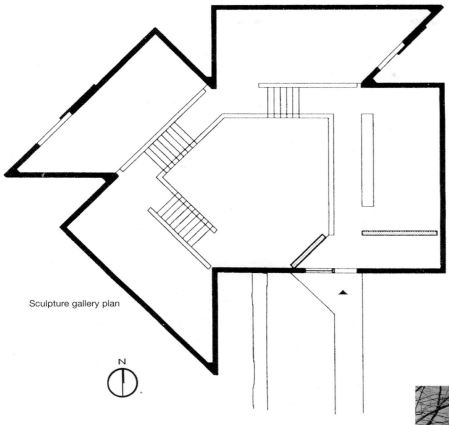

Sculpture gallery plan

N

Entry to sculpture gallery

The library/study is a composition of simple geometric shapes. The program consists of a table, chairs, bookshelves, and a fireplace.

Interior view of library/study

Library/study

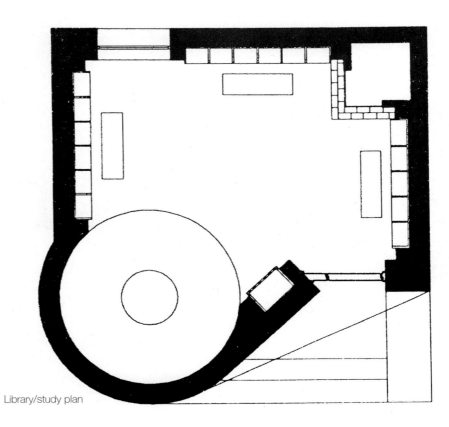

Library/study plan

Pavilion with water jet

The pavilion is a folly, set on the pond below the Glass House, positioned so that access requires a healthy jump from shore. It is roughly a pinwheel of rectangular platforms in plan. The problem of turning a corner when using a series of columns around the perimeter of a structure, known since the time of the ancient Greeks, is explored through the use of pre-cast concrete arches.

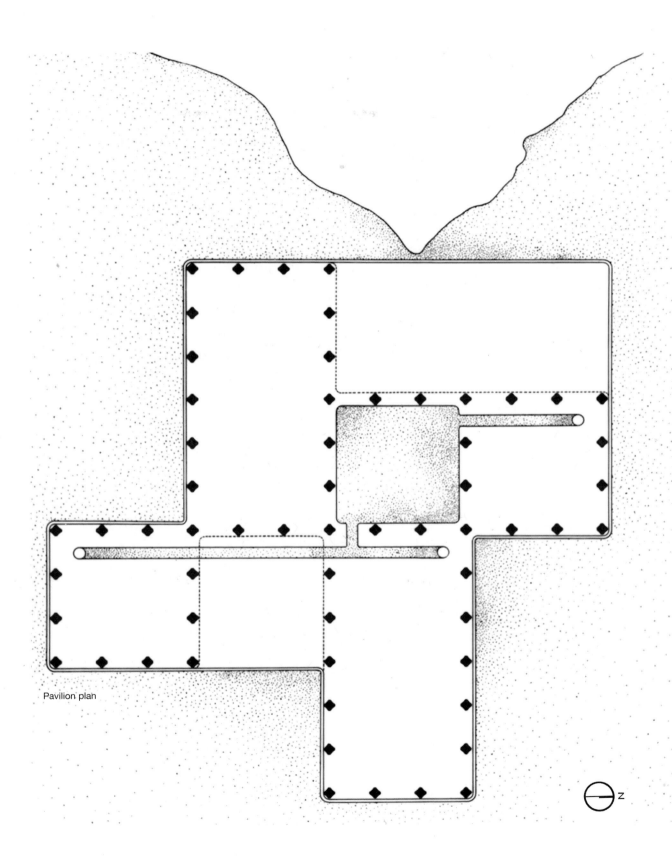

Pavilion plan

z

Lincoln Kirstein Tower

A purely sculptural piece, the Lincoln Kirstein tower is also a demonstration of the physiological relationship between art and the observer. It just about tempts the visitor to scale it. Mr. Johnson supposedly climbed it on occasion.

Gate house

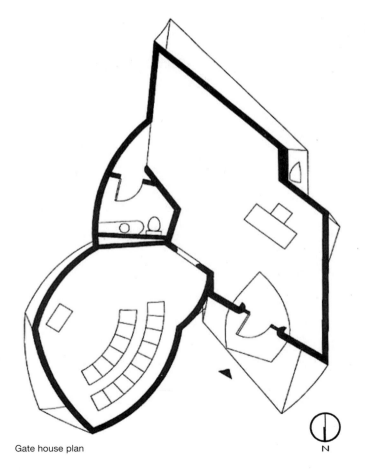
Gate house plan

The gate house, or "Monsta" as Philip Johnson affectionately called it, contains a desk, a small meeting room, and a bathroom. The walls and roof are of the same material, and there is only one vertical surface in the building.

Side of house. Living room with huge pane of fixed glass.

"The modern world has no tradition for its eight-hour day, its electric light, its central heating, its water supply, or any of its technical methods. One can roundly damn the whole of our age; one can commiserate with, or dissociate oneself from, or hope to transform the men and women who have lost their mental equilibrium in the vortex of modern life—but I do not believe that to decorate their homes with traditional gables and dormers helps them in the least. On the contrary, this only widens the gulf between appearance and reality and removes them still further from that ideal equilibrium which is, or should be, the ultimate object of all thought and action."

MARCEL BREUER

KNIFFEN HOUSE

MARCEL BREUER AND ELIOT NOYES ARCHITECTS

1949

Marcel Breuer designed a prototypical house that was built and temporarily displayed in the garden of the Museum of Modern Art. This house may be the closest realization of the ideal he exhibited there. As an example of his "bi-nuclear" designs, the children's bedrooms and the master bedroom were distinctly separated.

The house was demolished.

Upper floor: the master bedroom overlooks living room below

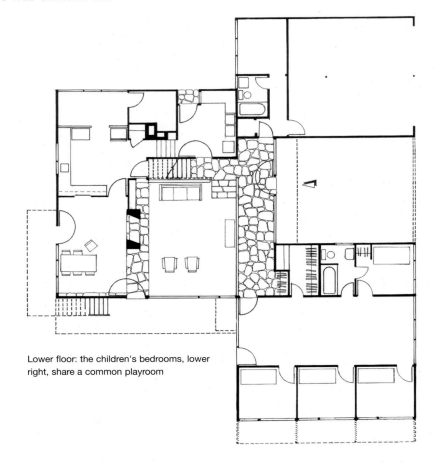

Lower floor: the children's bedrooms, lower right, share a common playroom

59

Rear of house with sliding window partly opened

JOHANSEN HOUSE
JOHN JOHANSEN ARCHITECT
1949

John Johansen

John Johansen designed the main living space on the first floor and placed the bedrooms in a half-exposed basement level. The living room wall facing the back yard was almost entirely glass and featured a huge sliding window. It has been said that, on occasion, Johansen would take a running jump out of the second-story window, spinning once in midair before landing on his feet on the front lawn.

The house was demolished.

by Mary Davis Gillies

it's an UPSIDE-DOWN house

*"We wanted to live up with the trees, not under them.
We wanted the feeling of being suspended in space,
so we put the living area upstairs and bedrooms below"*

McCALLS, June 1952

61

Rendering by John Johansen

VIEW FROM SOUTH

J.McL.J. 5/17/49

. HOUSE   NEW CANAAN .CONN.

"We wanted to live up in the trees, not under them. We wanted the feeling of being suspended in space, so we put the living area upstairs and the bedrooms below. The idea for our house came to us as we walked across a field toward the distant view and said, "Let us be here—on a floating platform at one with the landscape. Let us be a part of nature instead of intruding upon it."

JOHN JOHANSEN

"It's kind of sad, but you can understand that a child or a grandchild has to do their own thing. One approach is to give everything to the house, the best for the house, regardless of who is living in it. That means to change your life, somehow restrict yourself to living in a house which is a generation back or so. I wouldn't want my son, who is an architect, to live in my house. I'd rather tear it down. I want him to do his own house.

"Then this is the other view, the expression that the occupant is far more important. My wife says that houses are much too important to be left into the hands of architects. Because it's an autobiography. That's why I built my house with my own hands. It's mine and I can burn it down when it's all over.

"There is some kind of tribe in Indonesia or somewhere that identifies the occupant with the building they have lived in all their life to such an extent that when the occupant dies they systematically burn all the buildings. It's poor real estate, but a very tender idea."

JOHN JOHANSEN

Back of house

"I mistrust 'brilliancy' and 'taste.' The 'brilliant' work may flow too easily, trusting too much what the master already knows, what he already can do … The search for fundamentals often demands some self-destruction, some throwing away of mental provisions, some sacrifice. The resulting work will be less polished, less 'brilliant,' probably less pretty—but perhaps more important. One will acknowledge this: the fact that the purely aesthetical is transcended by the search towards something greater."

MARCEL BREUER

MILLS HOUSE

MARCEL BREUER ARCHITECT *1949*

The living room and dining room of this modest house utilized large expanses of fixed glass facing the back yard. The bedrooms were arranged around a common playroom, which was little more than a wide hallway. The brise soleil created patterns of shadows along the rear facade.

The house was demolished.

"The sun has to be reflected before it is trapped behind glass to fill the inside with radiant heat. The sun control device has to be on the outside of the building, an element of the façade, an element of architecture. And because this device is important, it may develop into as characteristic a form as the Doric column…"

MARCEL BREUER

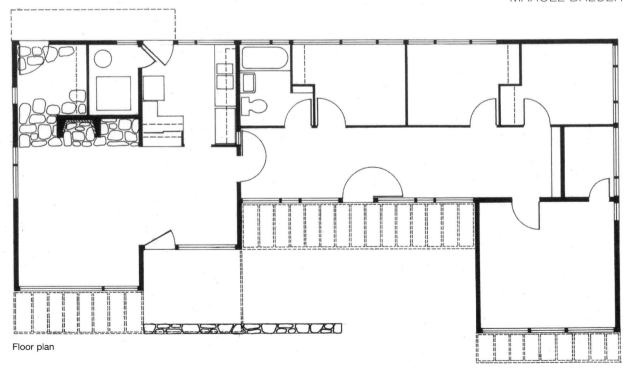

Floor plan

HOUSE for Mr & Mrs PETER DUN
NEW CANAAN, CONN.

Rendering by John Johansen

"For my early, low budget wooden houses, I devised very inexpensive detailing for door and window trim. These were cut from stock lumber, i.e., nominal 2"x 6" and 2" x 8". Although at first roughly fitted together, they were later articulated so as to come together neatly, properly and continually throughout an entire house—interior and exterior. My concern changed, however, from that of direct and early construction to that of perfectionist and tasteful detail, influenced at that time by Mies van der Rohe."

JOHN JOHANSEN

DUNHAM HOUSE
JOHN JOHANSEN ARCHITECT *1950*

John Johansen designed a series of houses based on the square. This one is an "H" in plan with the kitchen, bathrooms, and utility room in the center.

The house was demolished.

"I suppose these start with a perfect square. I was delighted to see how functional a house you could design within the limitations of strict geometries, or strict symmetries. I really feel that exhilaration at putting them together."

JOHN JOHANSEN

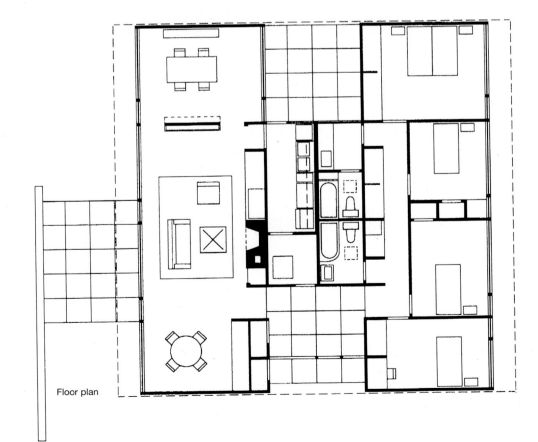

Floor plan

HOUSE for Mr & Mrs GORDON BAR
NEW CANAAN, CONN.
—II—
JOHN MAC-L. JOHANSEN ARCHITE
NEW CANAAN, CONN.

Rendering by John Johansen

"It was a very vivid time. We got out of school and we were just ecstatic, this open field. We were the ones to have been chosen, a few of us, to be at Harvard, and what we could do with it, and of course greatly to the credit of the school and Gropius was to say: This was not a style, don't look at what we're doing. We'll give you the tools and the thinking and the approach. We want you to do your own thing. That must be made clear."

JOHN JOHANSEN

BARLOW HOUSE
JOHN JOHANSEN ARCHITECT   *1950*

Model of spray-form house

Few records of John Johansen's houses remain. He lost many original drawings in a fire, and many of the houses have been demolished. This is one of the modest houses in the "square" series. While Johansen was creating the square series, he was also experimenting with organically shaped concrete structures like the one at left.

"Strict geometries never moved me: I've fallen into them. This particular series of houses, neo-Palladian, which was six or eight of them at that time, was an effort to get away from the Bauhaus teaching and the stern principles of the founders.

"They were symmetrical indeed. So that's an admission of mine. That's my neo-classical period. I had to free myself. I had to, after the War, go to Europe, study Palladio, see those dazzling things that were never mentioned really during my schooling at Harvard. It was all severance with the past. You don't look back. You only look forward. Very little breadth or deviation from that, or we felt there was not. So our second generation is an outburst of diversity, huge diversity.

"This, then, was an effort of mine, these strictly symmetrical plans, to get my outlet. Then I got over it. At the same time I was doing these I was doing sprayed concrete, which leads to all these rounded things."

JOHN JOHANSEN

View to living room

View from street

"The compact, offset volumes of the Hodgson house are expressed in a tripartite elevation of brick and glass, topped by a steel cornice. So the house clearly owes a debt to Mies. But its plan also echoes those of Pompeian villas. The entry foyer of the house opens on axis to a glass enclosed courtyard surrounded by day time living areas, with a secondary axis leading to the bedroom pavilion. The brick used in construction of the house is a blue-gray cobalt spot."

ARCHITECTURAL RECORD, March 1953

HODGSON HOUSE
PHILIP JOHNSON ARCHITECT
1951

Back of chimney and passage to courtyard

Contained within a simple shape, this house uses elegant materials in a restrained manner. The considerable glass area is balanced by the visual weight of the brick walls. From some rooms it is possible to see across the courtyard, straight through rooms in another wing of the house, and into the landscape beyond.

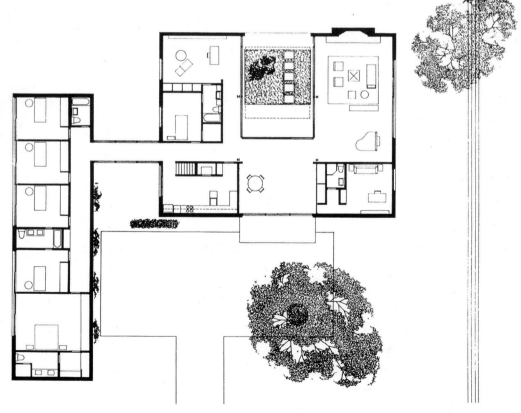
Floor plan

East side of house

Southwest corner of house showing viewing platform

STACKPOLE HOUSE
ELIOT NOYES ARCHITECT
1951

The second-floor wood-framed bedroom wing was delicately perched on slender steel columns, and slightly overlapped the stone-clad first floor. The shifting planar volumes of first and second floor created a classic modern DeStijl effect.

The house was demolished.

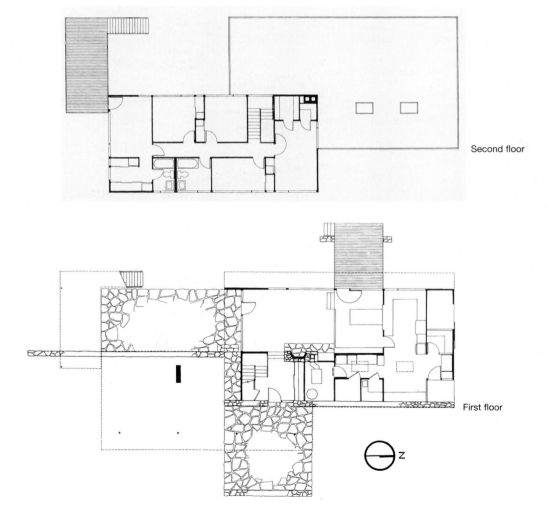

Second floor

First floor

Rear of house; the pool and guest house were later additions

"'What' asks the layman 'do the houses of Johnson and Gores have in common? And why is Noyes' Bremer house, for example, way up in the air and his Ault house flat on the ground? Why did Breuer build his first New Canaan house as a light wooden box balanced on a small base and his second as a monumental-looking house of stone? Why do some houses have deep overhangs and others none? Do roofs have to be flat? Isn't there some simple way of getting the 'hang' of these modern houses just as there is with Colonial or Greek revival houses? The answer, of course, is 'no.'"

HOUSE & HOME, January 1953

BREMER HOUSE

ELIOT NOYES ARCHITECT *1951*

Reminiscent of Le Corbusiers' Villa Savoye, the first floor of the Bremer house is raised on slim columns, or pilotis, with the main living area upstairs. A generous, partially covered terrace extends from the living areas and master bedroom.

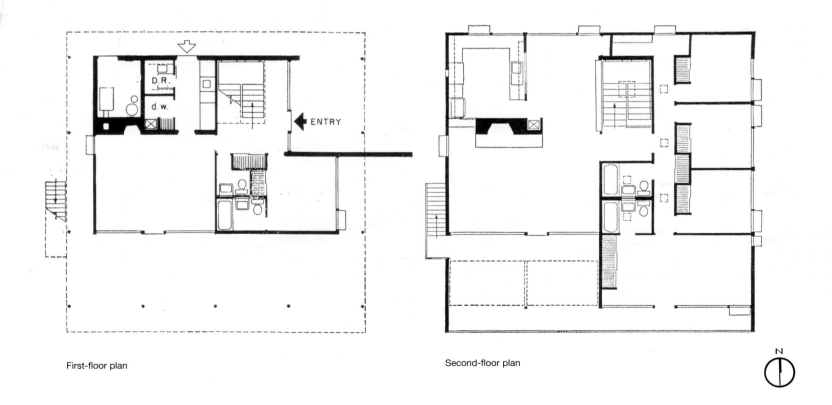

First-floor plan

Second-floor plan

N

Marcel Breuer on the terrace of the Bremer House

Interior stair seen from outside

Colors which you can hear with ears;
Sounds to see with eyes;
The void you touch with your elbows;
The taste of space on your tongue;
The fragrance of dimensions;
The juice of stone.
MARCEL BREUER

Entry

"We 'modern' architects don't hate tradition—the opposite is true. I admire it and have traveled in old countries to look up old buildings, to study and photograph them, to analyze and discover their spirit. But I cannot use traditional methods when I want to build a house, although sometimes I wish I could. It is a more difficult task and a rather thankless one, this direct approach. But it is also more exciting."

MARCEL BREUER

BREUER HOUSE 2

MARCEL BREUER ARCHITECT *1951*

In contrast to Breuer's first house in New Canaan, this house sits firmly on the ground. Perhaps inspired by the stone walls left by farmers that trace rectangular patterns through this part of Connecticut, Breuer used stone as a primary building material. As seen in the floor plan, the walls of his house seem to spin off into the landscape. The planar effect of the vertical surfaces is emphasized: no wall material ever seems to turn a corner.

View from the street

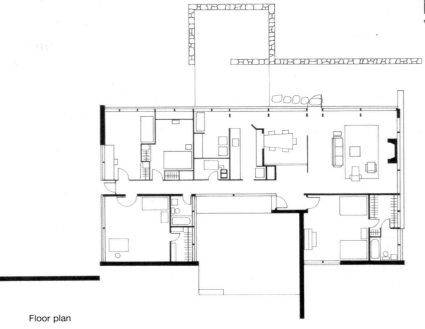
Floor plan

"God knows, I am all for informal living and for architecture in support of and as background for this, but we won't sidestep the instinct towards achievement—a human instinct indeed. The most contrasting elements of our nature should be brought to happiness at the same time, in the same work, and in the most definite way. The drive to experiment is there, together with and in contrast to the warm joy of security at the fireplace. The crystallic quality of an unbroken white flat slab is there, together with and in contrast to the rough, 'texture-y' quality of natural wood or broken stone."

MARCEL BREUER

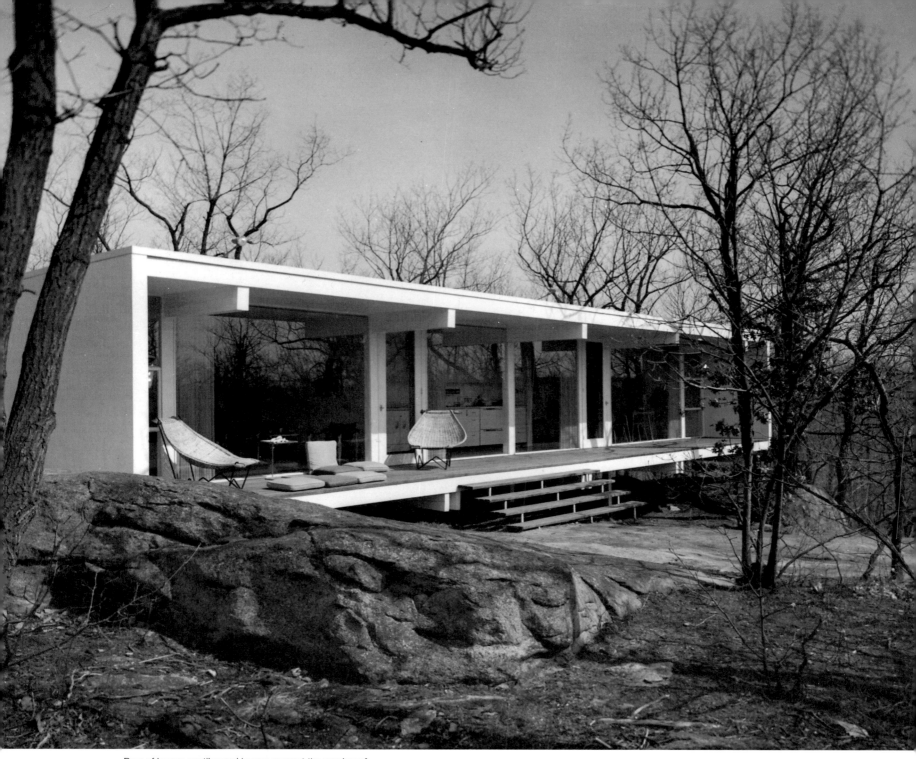

Rear of house: cantilevered beams support the porch roof

"Modernism is more like a spirit than a style."   JOHN BLACK LEE

LEE HOUSE 1

JOHN BLACK LEE ARCHITECT *1952*

This white box hovers over its moss-covered rocky site. The simple rhythm of the structure of the house is expressed in the dropped beams of the ceiling. Three sides of the house have no roof overhang; one side has a deep overhang that creates a porch sheltering a wall of glass.

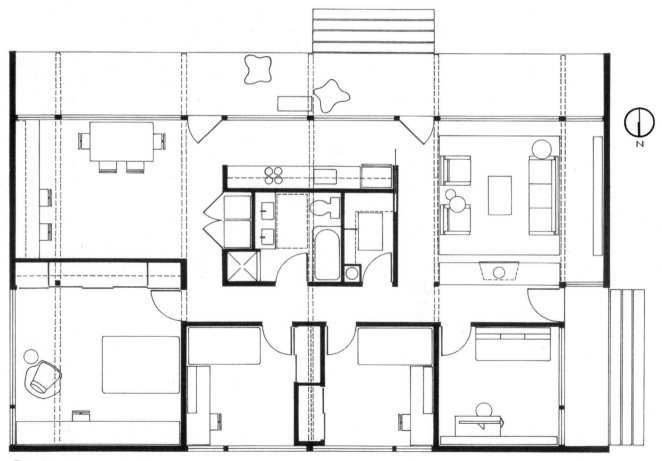

Floor plan

Approach to house

The stark simplicity of this house creates a heightened sense of appreciation for its untamed site. It does not attempt to burrow into or lock itself onto the ground, but instead politely and gently rests above the terrain, perched on a dramatic rock outcropping.

Side of house

Covered porch

Architect's home office

Living room

A compact core contains the laundry, kitchen, and sky-lit bathrooms. Under the core, a small stone base supports the house. The kitchen counter (top right) is along an interior wall. The wall opposite the kitchen is entirely glass.

Bedroom

The floor-to-ceiling windows in the master bedroom overlook a tremendous drop in the rocky landscape directly below.

South side of house

RILEY HOUSE
CHAUNCEY RILEY ARCHITECT
1952

This house was sited at the top of a rocky outcropping at one end of a long narrow property, with an open field in the middle and the far end anchored by a natural pond. Because it was positioned so far to one end of the site, the view from the house gave the impression of a much larger property, with the field below and the pond in the distance.

The house was demolished.

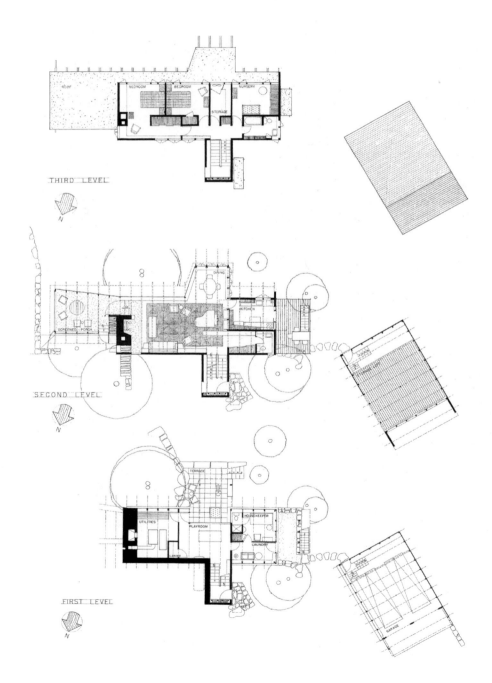

THIRD LEVEL

N

SECOND LEVEL

N

FIRST LEVEL

N

West side of house

The path from the garage to the house used some of the existing stone outcroppings as steps. It was a three-story house, with the floating staircase doing double duty as a library. The screen porch, tucked behind the fireplace, had one wall of glass that reinforced the impression of sitting outdoors.

Side view of breakfast nook

Living room

Stairs to second floor

93

View from street

IRWIN HOUSE

VICTOR CHRIST-JANER ARCHITECT

1952

View from back yard

This house has a simple rectangular shape and is clad in natural siding.

Victor Christ-Janer was known for his use of words, convincing his clients to use his services through the power of sheer persuasion. He was also known to interrupt work-related activities of his office staff just to lecture upon his theories.

"New Canaan hasn't made up its mind yet. While there are still some wild and somewhat incoherent cries in the local paper against *all* the houses, 1100 people, on the other hand, came to visit and explore during the first 'open house' day."

HOLIDAY, August 1952

Original Campbell house

CAMPBELL HOUSE
JOHN JOHANSEN ARCHITECT
1952

This was originally one of John Johansen's square houses, with interior courtyards creating an "H" in plan. The roof is supported by four main carrying beams, and the space between these beams is filled with glass to create a clerestory. Although renovated and added to by another architect for his own use, the house retains much of its original spirit.

Floor plan with additions and alterations by Alan Goldberg

Original house, painted

"One benefit of living through the renovation was that we didn't have to sweep the floors for a year."

ALAN GOLDBERG

Additions with original house visible within

Present Goldberg House with entry still visible on the left

Architect Alan Goldberg with his children during renovations

"I once asked my children if living through the renovation had scarred them in some way."

ALAN GOLDBERG

Rear of house

Living room and dining room after renovation

Front of the house

Northwest corner

"Some traditionalists (in New Canaan and elsewhere) think that modern architects ought to 'go back where they came from'; others think that people who build modern houses are rather vulgar 'strangers' from New York who have no feeling for the beauty of the New England countryside, don't understand the wealth of the colonial tradition and represent the most Philistine element in our materialistic society.

"Some modernists, on the other hand, think that all traditionalists are reactionary snobs; others think that modern architecture is a delayed creative extension of the New England tradition and will soon be recognized as such: still others just want to be left alone to work out esthetic problems that they feel are still far from a final solution."

HOUSE & HOME, January 1953

BALL HOUSE

PHILIP JOHNSON ARCHITECT *1953*

Mies van der Rohe's courtyard houses influenced this modest rectangular house. The primary axis of the house is crossed by a secondary axis passing through the main living space. This secondary axis is purely spatial and is defined only by a wall of windows and doors on either side of the room and the terraces outside.

Floor plan

Side of house with floor-to-ceiling sliding door

"An event is defined as an action that was taken at a certain time and place. That is what the strict definition of an event is. If they hadn't come together it wouldn't be an event. This is an event. The place is New Canaan. The time was then. Everything went around that. And it won't happen again. It may be another event somewhere else, but not again here. It's unique and it's limited in time and it's there and it's over. It's interesting to trace what the forces were, the circumstances that came together to make that event, which wouldn't have happened ten years later or earlier. It's a kind of magic."

JOHN JOHANSEN

GOODE HOUSE

JOHN JOHANSEN ARCHITECT *1953*

The main floor of this simple, geometrically shaped house was positioned over a recessed, partially buried lower level, and cantilevered out on all four sides. A clerestory brought light into the center of the house. Monumental, open-riser exterior stairs, without any railings, seemed to only lightly touch the house.

The house was demolished.

North east corner

Rendering

"One thinks that the latest work is the best that you have done as an architect. You ride along like that and forget all this stuff. Then I see these renderings and I think: 'That's not bad, probably a lot better than I'm doing now.'"

JOHN JOHANSEN

Back of house

"The effect from the house—quite opposite of my glass house—is that of a cage. No indoor-outdoor nonsense. The 15 foot ceilings free the view into the high hickories that surround the house which at night make fantastic traceries against the black sky."

PHILIP JOHNSON

WILEY HOUSE

PHILIP JOHNSON ARCHITECT *1953*

This house has two equal and opposite axes. The first is the stone base, which is exposed down the slope of the site and contains the bedrooms and bathrooms. The second axis is the double-height glass enclosure for the kitchen and living areas, which is turned ninety degrees from the base. The top part of the house is as much void as the base is solid.

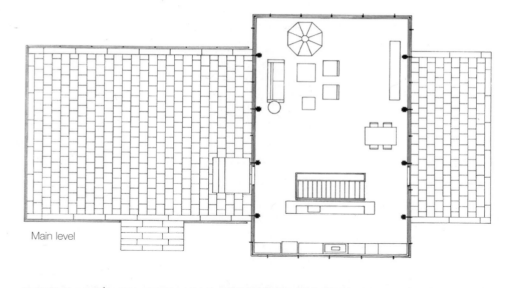

Main level

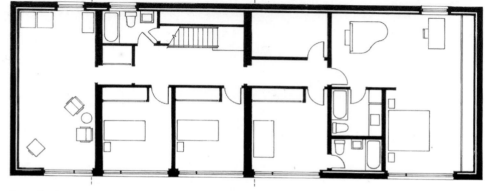

Lower level

Living room and dining area

Rear of the house, with awnings

"Question: Do only cranks live in modern houses?"

"Answer: Modern-house owners seem no more or less cranky than other suburbanites."

HOUSE & HOME, January 1953

House from driveway

DICKENSON HOUSE
JOHN JOHANSEN ARCHITECT
1953

In the Dickenson house, the simple geometric shapes of Johansen's earlier houses were stretched into a cross. The clerestory became much larger and defined the entire middle of the house. The main floor was perched over a half-buried lower floor; access to it was by wide stairs without handrails.

The house was demolished.

"As one New Canaan traditionalist put it recently: "Who knows—perhaps when we celebrate our 300th anniversary, we'll be pointing proudly to these houses and telling the world that here, in this little town, we helped create a new architectural tradition. It would be too bad, anyway, if all we had to show for the next 150 years would be more of the same."

HOUSE & HOME, January 1953

Demolition of Dickenson house prior to construction of a speculative house

View through courtyard from back yard

NOYES HOUSE 2

ELIOT NOYES ARCHITECT

1954

This courtyard house has two massive stone walls framing two glass wings. The only way to get from the bedroom wing to the living room wing is to pass outdoors under a covered roof.

The courtyard contains Alexander Calder's sculpture, "The Black Beast."

Floor plan

Bedroom side of house

View from street

"I think of details in two senses. There are first the details of joints, connections, the attachment of different materials to each other, the turning of corners, the physical relating of parts of the building to each other. But I also think of larger special elements as details—such things as stairs and fireplaces—in which there are of course numerous details in the other sense. In each case the architect has a useful and expressive architectural device. In a way, such architectural details are the architecture, but details alone—no matter how thought out or how consistent—cannot make architecture. Such details must play their part in relation to the over-all concept and character of the building, and are the means by which the architect may underline his main idea, reinforce it, echo it, intensify it or dramatize it.

"I like details of both sorts to be simple, practical, efficient, articulate, appropriate, neat, handsome, and contributory to the clarity of all relationships.

"The converse of this is that the spectator may observe and enjoy details, and find in them an extension of his experience and understanding of the architecture. In them he should be able to read, or least see reflected, the character and spirit of the entire building—as to see the universe in a grain of sand."

ELIOT NOYES

Lliving room

Approach to house

RAYFORD HOUSE

FRANK LLOYD WRIGHT ARCHITECT

1956

The original plan of this house was changed soon after completion to incorporate a sweeping loggia leading to a circular conservatory and covered parking. Later additions provided more living space and created an enclosed courtyard.

Although the primary building material is concrete block, the use of mahogany exterior trim and interior paneling creates a warm elegance.

An outdoor terrace completes the elliptical shape in plan. The original design called for screening this terrace, but this was never carried out. An elliptical pool was later added below the terrace, which overlooks the Noroton River.

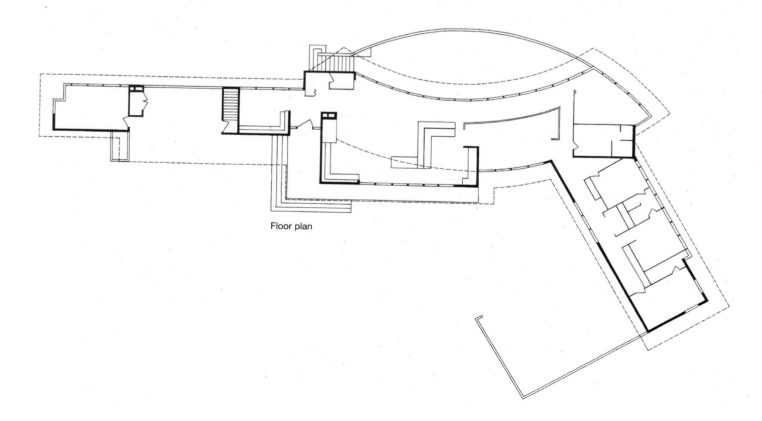

Floor plan

Living room with addition at left

Terrace overlooking pool

Landis Gores revered Frank Lloyd Wright as his personal inspiration and wrote this epitaph as a tribute:

IN MEMORIAM: FRANK LLOYD WRIGHT
Kings do not shout in the market; nor, once crowned,
Pass time of day with hucksters but sooner bide
In shadows regal while forced to stand aside
For passing petty princelings that abound
In shriveling times to claim new empires found
New secrets solved, all truth from its matrix pried:
But, throne restored, spread splendor multiplied
Past count from vaults of gold on gold compound.
Kings do not bow; but kings must also die,
No less than lesser men who quietly pass
From view in pale phantasmagoric stream.
Kings too meet Fate; and yet to me it seemed
True kings in word and work so far surpass
Mutability, that Time itself stood by.

Front of house today

Back of house today

Front of house: a glen of tall pines creates a serene environment

LEE HOUSE 2
JOHN BLACK LEE ARCHITECT
1956

The symmetrical plan is wrapped with a covered porch and topped by a clerestory. The architect Toshiko Mori recently renovated the house. She replaced the exterior wood columns with brushed metal sections and raised the height of the clerestory, but preserved the floor plan.

Porch after renovation.

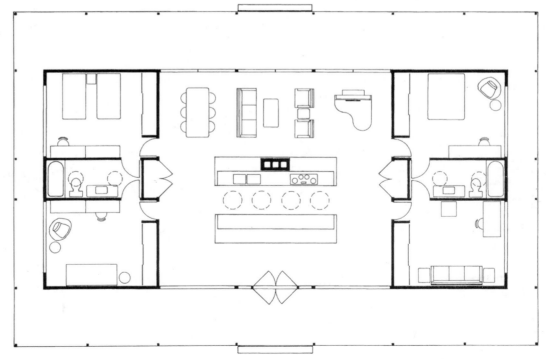

Floor plan

Entry

Clerestory windows raise the ceiling over the middle of the house

Kitchen

Mr. and Mrs. Lee in kitchen

Living room bridging the river

WARNER HOUSE
JOHN JOHANSEN ARCHITECT   *1956*

Johansen took a dramatic turn away from his series of simple square houses with the Warner house. This house breaks all the rules of modernity: it is symmetrical, it has an expressive roof profile, and it is far from Spartan in its materials and finishes. Yet, it is undeniably modern.

The dining room and living room are actually built as a bridge over a small stream. A modest waterfall under the house creates a constant pleasant sound.

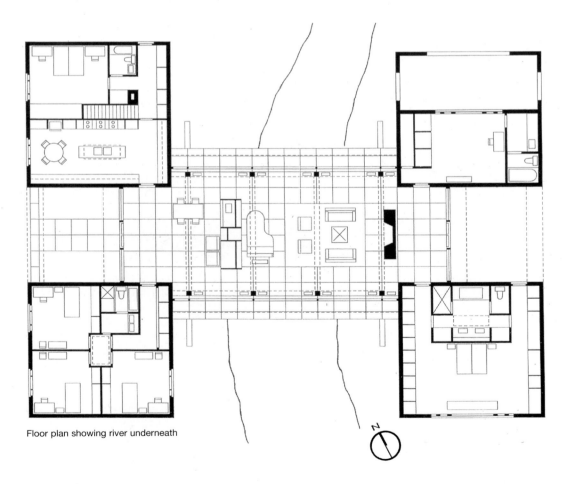

Floor plan showing river underneath

"Modernity is timeless. Its opposite is conservatism. That's also timeless. The play of those two, it will always come back, of course always there, in larger or smaller currents. I have a great expectation for a new birth of modern. First, a recognition among the young for Breuer and those whom they don't even know. They don't know me very much. Then to recreate their own awakening, their own period of time. I feel very strongly about it."

JOHN JOHANSEN

Living room

View from river

"This idyllic house blends two strong, yet often quite divergent trends: a rational, regulated neo-Palladian influence dominates the plan and balanced design; a decided romantic turn is obvious in the setting, bridge-like construction, vaulted roof, terracotta-colored stucco exterior (patterned with bas relief's)—and gargoyles for downspouts. Finishes throughout are rich in tone: gold leaf on the vaulted ceiling, terrazzo floors, ebonized wood cabinets."

THE SECOND TREASURY OF CONTEMPORARY HOUSES, 1957

Back of house

Front of house

BOISSONAS HOUSE

PHILIP JOHNSON ARCHITECT

1956

The plan of the house is a series of squares; some interior, some exterior. The volume is a collection of cubes, some single, some double or quadruple. The monumental corners and freestanding columns carry a white cornice beam around the exterior. Brick is not used so much as a weight-bearing building material but as a decorative surface treatment.

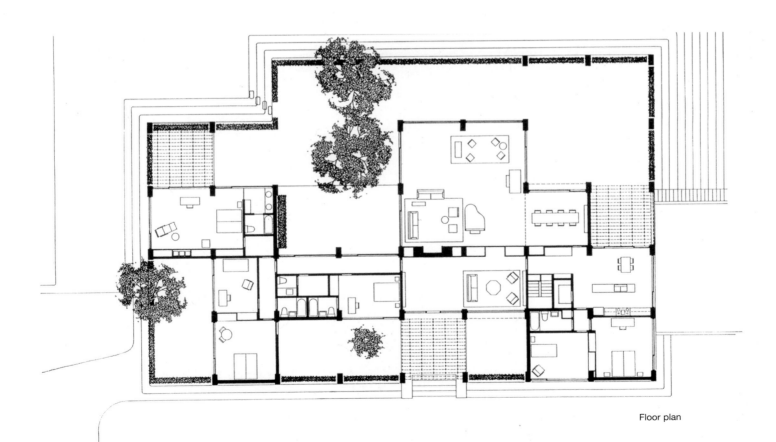

Floor plan

Pergola

"As far as my own work was concerned, I was a devoted disciple of Mies and of the Style. The Style lasted clearly through the 1950s, but then I got bored with it. My reaction was an anti-father one. Anti-Mies. Anti-modern. I joined in with what Robert A. M. Stern and Robert Venturi were doing, putting forth the continuity of history as something that could be learned from. Being an historian first and an architect afterward, I found the idea appealing. I jumped at Venturi's book, Complexity and Contradiction in Architecture, in the early sixties. But I'm a jumper-arounder anyhow. I was interested in Schinkel, Classicism, and Ledoux before I was interested in modern architecture."

PHILIP JOHNSON

Rear of house

Side of house: front door is at right

SMALLEN HOUSE

HUGH SMALLEN ARCHITECT
1957

This house is a trapezoidal white box with one wall almost entirely of glass. The terrace runs the width of the house and ends with a stone sitting wall. The opposite side has two levels of ribbon windows. A wood bridge leads to the front door.

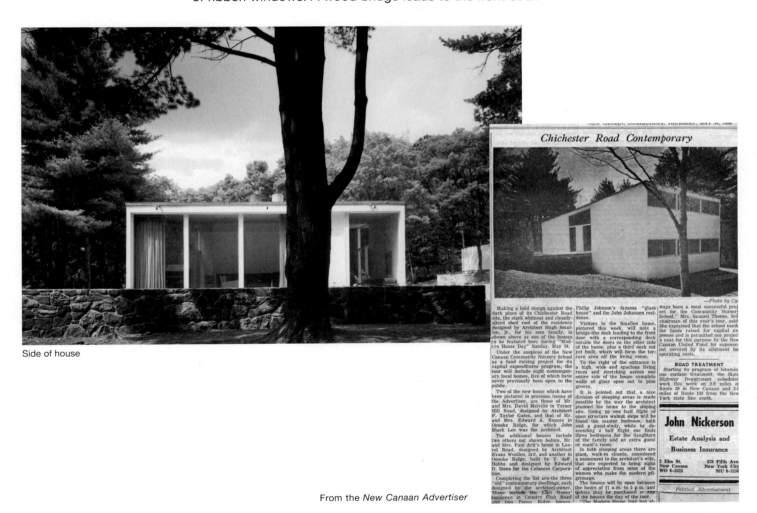

Side of house

Chichester Road Contemporary

—Photo by Cy

Making a bold design against the dark pines of its Chichester Road site, the stark whiteness and cleanly-sliced shed roof of the residence designed by Architect Hugh Smallen, Jr., for his own family, is shown above as one of the houses to be featured here during "Modern House Day" Sunday, May 24.

Under the auspices of the New Canaan Community Nursery School as a fund raising project for its capital expenditures program, the tour will include eight contemporary local homes, five of which have never previously been open to the public.

Two of the new homes which have been pictured in previous issues of the Advertiser, are those of Mr. and Mrs. David Melville in Turner Hill Road, designed by Architect F. Taylor Gates, and that of Mr. and Mrs. Edward A. Rogers in Oenoke Ridge, for which John Black Lee was the architect.

The additional houses include two others not shown before, Mr. and Mrs. Paul Arlt's home in Laurel Road, designed by Architect Evans Woollen, 3rd, and another in Oenoke Ridge, built by T. deF. Hobbs and designed by Edward D. Stone for the Celanese Corporation.

Completing the list are the three "old" contemporary dwellings, each designed by the architect-owner. These include the Eliot Noyes' residence in Country Club Road and two Ponus Ridge homes,

Philip Johnson's famous "glass house" and the John Johansen residence.

Visitors to the Smallen home, pictured this week, will note a bridge-like deck leading to the front door with a corresponding deck outside the doors on the other side of the house, plus a third deck not yet built, which will form the terrace area off the living room.

To the right of the entrance is a high, wide and spacious living room and stretching across one entire side of the house complete walls of glass open out to pine groves.

It is pointed out that a nice division of sleeping areas is made possible by the way the architect planned his home to the sloping site. Going up one half flight of open structure walnut steps will be found the master bedroom, bath and a guest-study, while by descending a half flight one finds three bedrooms for the daughters of the family and an extra guest or maid's room.

In both sleeping areas there are giant, walk-in closets, considered a monument to the architect's wife, that are expected to bring sighs of appreciation from most of the women who make the modern pilgrimage.

The houses will be open between the hours of 11 a.m. to 5 p.m. and tickets may be purchased at any of the houses the day of the tour. "The Modern Home Day has al-

ways been a most successful project for the Community Nursery School," Mrs. Samuel Thorne, 3rd, chairman of this year's tour, said. She explained that the school needs the funds raised for capital expenses and is permitted one project a year for this purpose by the New Canaan United Fund for expenses not covered by its allotment for operating costs.

ROAD TREATMENT

Starting its program of bituminous surface treatment, the State Highway Department scheduled work this week on 2.9 miles of Route 39 in New Canaan and 2.1 miles of Route 123 from the New York state line south.

John Nickerson

Estate Analysis and Business Insurance

2 Elm St.   579 Fifth Ave.
New Canaan   New York City
WO 6-3555   MU 8-2156

Political Advertisement

From the *New Canaan Advertiser*

Cantilevered patio and balcony

MILLS HOUSE
HUGH SMALLEN ARCHITECT *1957*

The stone path from the driveway leads to a wood balcony overlooking the moss covered rocky landscape. The balcony takes a sharp right into the house and looks over the double-height volume of the living room below. The house was recently renovated: the garage was converted into a master suite, the kitchen relocated and opened to a dining area, and materials and finishes updated throughout, but the main living room space remains essentially the same.

"Working with a particularly difficult site problem, the architects have produced an effective and dramatic solution by designing this two-story house to rest midway down a steep, rocky slope."

THE SECOND TREASURY OF
CONTEMPORARY HOUSES, 1957

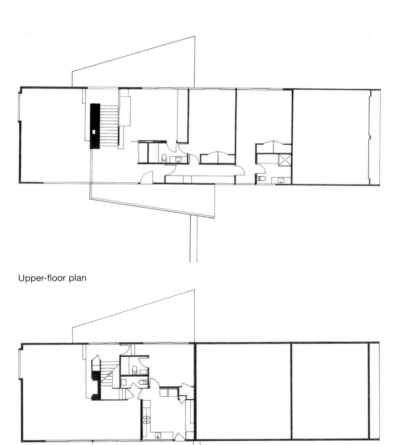

Upper-floor plan

Lower-floor plan

Front of house

Living room with triple-hung window, after renovation

View from living room, after renovation

The upstairs balcony continues directly through to the outdoors. The living room extends to a terrace bordered by a rocky landscape that shelters it from the street.

Front of house

Rear of house

CELANESE HOUSE

EDWARD DURRELL STONE ARCHITECT *1959*

This house mysteriously conceals itself behind a wood screen of diamonds and triangles. The only fenestration visible at the approach is the front door. The front and back of the house are nearly identical, wrapped in a lattice from the ground to the overhanging roof. The primary source of light in the interior is from the huge pyramidal skylights.

Living room with skylight

Dining room with skylight

Corner view of pool house

144

IRWIN POOL HOUSE
LANDIS GORES ARCHITECT
1960

Interior of pool house

View of fireplace

Landis Gores kept a journal about the design and construction of the Irwin pool house. He noted: "The temperature was rising in more ways than one as we pushed to ready the pool house for the summer season. The caretaker was obliged almost daily to shoo off the curious.

"But then in mid-September an unexpected invitation to a definitive house-warming. Arriving with Pam some minutes after the hour specified, I was flabbergasted to behold three or four dozen guests standing assembled while Jane (Irwin) announced the arrival of the guest of honor. Had I thus understood the occasion I would have moved Heaven and Earth to be precisely on time.

"A dozen old acquaintances, and from Philip Johnson's list, Connie and Lajko Breuer, Molly and El Noyes, Mary and Ed Barnes, Paul Rudolph, Doug Haskell, Peter Blake, I. M. Pei. A lovely party, flawlessly produced by a client and a friend who had become to me 'a true princess' in a world where so few have access to the purple and yet fewer know how to wear it in a truly regal fashion."

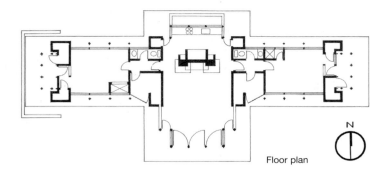

Floor plan

N

Front of house with additions by John Black Lee

TEAZE HOUSE

JOHN BLACK LEE ARCHITECT *1961*

The symmetrical massing of this house conceals the reality of the functions within: bedrooms to one side and living, dining and kitchen to the other. The closets and bookshelves along the entire front of the house projected at the top and the bottom, which made them appear as floating masses on both sides of the front door. The view on the facing page shows additions, designed by John Black Lee, that project further into the driveway. They have wood-slat walls with translucent plastic panels that admit light yet preserve privacy.

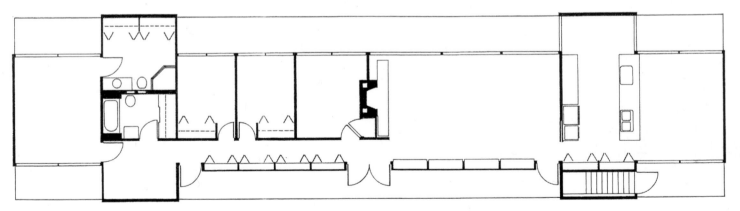

Floor plan before renovation

View across pond

McCARTHY HOUSE
ALLAN GELBIN ARCHITECT *1961*

The plan is roughly a series of triangles arranged in a pinwheel around the core of the house, which is marked with a triangular skylight. Steps down to the living room increase the height of this room, and a deck flows out and cantilevers over the pond below.

Kitchen

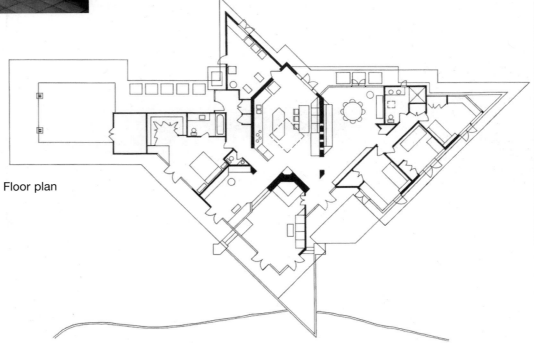

Floor plan

View from side showing bridge to front door

DeSILVER HOUSE

JOHN BLACK LEE ARCHITECT *1961*

Columns surround the house and support a second-floor balcony and the wide overhanging roof. This house was conceived as a "systems" house, a kit of parts designed to be quickly and efficiently constructed. John Black Lee sold copies of the design through the mail. Duplicates of this house may exist throughout the country.

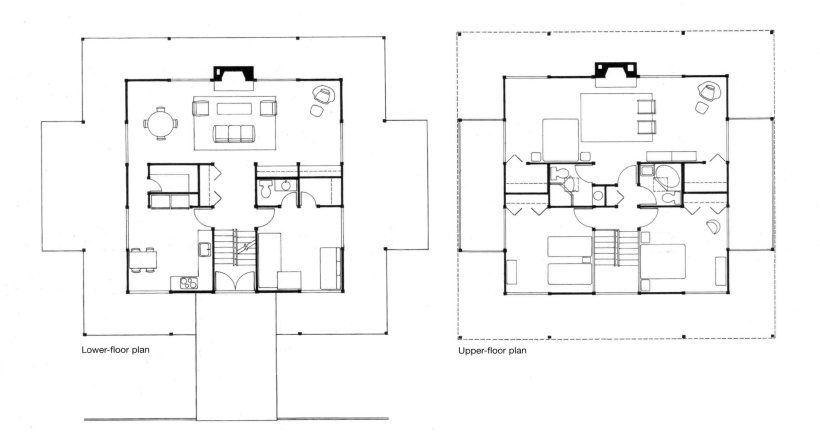

Lower-floor plan

Upper-floor plan

Couple observing construction progress

Architects have often felt the need to design a house so that it can be constructed with as few parts as possible for efficiency and economy. This house is an exploration of this concept. It is designed as a square within a square. The flat roof is supported by a series of slender columns that also support the second-floor balconies. Although the house was designed for efficiency of construction, the interior and exterior spaces are relatively luxurious.

Visitors arriving during one of the "modern house day" tours, date unknown

Living room

PARSONS HOUSE
HUGH SMALLEN ARCHITECT
1965

Seen from the street, this classic modern white box has a sharply angled windowless facade that follows the sloping terrain. Floor-to-ceiling glass walls provide a dramatic yet private view of the wooded site.

New York Times Magazine, July 25, 1965

Retaining wall with stairs built into landscape

DAY HOUSE

JOHN BLACK LEE ARCHITECT *1966*

Compared to Lee's earlier house designs, this house is large and the materials are luxurious. The enormous cantilevered roof is supported by brick piers. The procession to the front door reinforces the strict symmetry of the massing, and the formal interior double stair bisects a generous entry hall. Many exterior as well as interior doors are pocket doors.

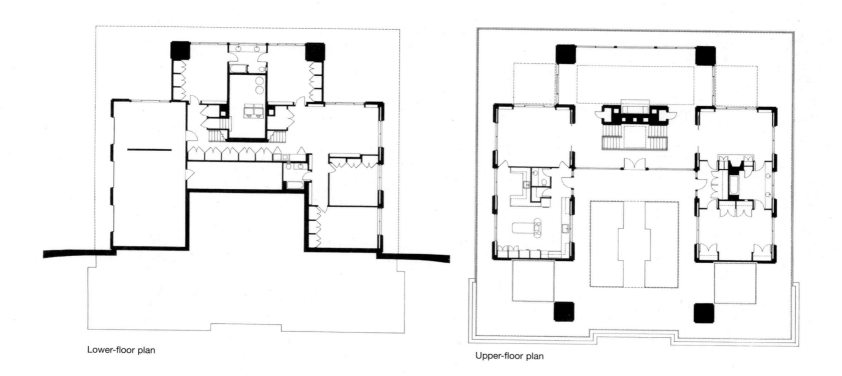

Lower-floor plan

Upper-floor plan

The monumentality of this house is created by the stepped base, the massive brick columns, the thick yet apparently weightless roof, and the symmetrical front facade. The courtyard approach to the double front doors reinforces the drama, while the light-colored brick and white cornice are coolly sophisticated.

Approach to house

Courtyard

View of house from the back

LUTHOLD HOUSE
ALLAN GELBIN ARCHITECT
1966

The entry to the house begins as a procession of rectilinear spaces, but as the visitor progresses through the house layers of circles open up and then become ellipses. The flat planar surfaces of the entry facade change to overlapping curves at the back of the house. The terrace cascades down to a swimming pool, which is built above a pond. The pond is defined by rough rocks on one side and a smooth curving concrete edge on the other. The play of shapes and materials, from the exterior through the interior, creates a dialogue between the natural and the man-made.

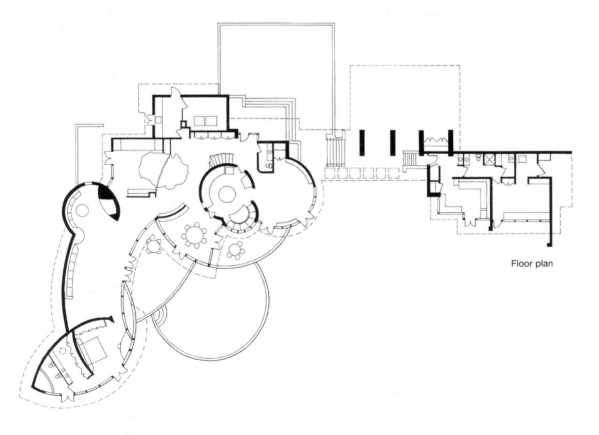

Floor plan

Dark stained mahogany defines the curving outer roof edges

Entrance courtyard

Second floor cantilevered over dining room

Doorway from dining room to terrace

IN MARCH 1952 A BRIEF ARTICLE APPEARED IN THE LOCAL NEWSPAPER, THE *NEW CANAAN ADVERTISER*, DESCRIBING A TALK PHILIP JOHNSON HAD GIVEN TO THE LOCAL KIWANIS CLUB. A READER SENT A RHYMING LETTER TO THE EDITOR EXPRESSING HIS VIEW OF THE MATTER, AND A SERIES OF LETTERS FOLLOWED BY OTHER WOULD-BE POETS. THE FRONT PAGE OF THE *ADVERTISER* READS, "PUBLISHED IN 'THE NEXT STATION TO HEAVEN' SINCE 1908."

CANTILEVER HEAVEN
OR
WEARING OUT YOUR WELCOME

I see by the Advertiser of March 6, Page 7, Column 4
That Mr. Philip (Glass House) Johnson, with modesty galore,
Let the Kiwanis in on the secret that New Canaan has become
    world famous
(He should have said notorious) because he and Eliot Noyes and
    Walter Gropius
And Landis Gores and John Johansen and Marcel Breuer and
    probably more as equally obnoxious
Have graciously condescended to settle here and ruin the country
    side with packing boxes
And partially-opened bureau drawers set on steel posts and
    stanchions
An architectural form as gracious as Sunoco service stations.

It seems to me there are about seventy-nine hundred out of our
    eight thousand population
That wish to hell that Harvard and the Modern Art Museum
Had provided padded cells for their brilliant graduate architects,
Complete with air-conditioned functions and cantilevered sundecks
Windowless, doorless, charmless and escape-proof.
We wouldn't care if Cambridge or 53rd Street were covered with
    one big flat roof
So long as Breuer, Gores, Johnson, Noyes, Johansen
Were under it instead of in the station next to heaven.

OGDEN GNASH-TEETH
March 13, 1952

ROUND ROBIN

In the interest that last week's quasi-rhymed broadside concerned the desecration of the New Canaan countryside may not go unanswered by at least a modest salvo, I have been delegated perhaps most unfortunately in view of the immediacy of involvement to submit you the following round robin Decalogue composed by the assembled guests at a dinner party within the town late last Saturday night.

    I must unequivocally disclaim either praise or blame for any more than my rationed share of the mortification; further, not another architect of any coloration was implicated while I for myself disdain to emulate last week's dubious example by taking refuge behind the skirts of petulant pseudonymity.

    I should like also to express appreciation of the stalwart unanimity (and sic) of the present contributor even if at the expense of mellifluous transition from one line to the next.

We see by the Advertiser of March 13, Page 4, Column 6,
That in the craw of Mr. Gnash-Teeth modern architecture sticks
Allergic to glass, steel, bureau drawers and cantilevers
A stuffy old stuffed-shirt with grey myopia fever
Undulant, ruminant, tobacco on his vest,
Grandiloquent grandson of a grandson of the best,
Who latterly has failed, we fear to grasp in the slightest
That that which was found good in the past is no longer today the
    object of affection of the brightest
That pigeons chalk his widow's walk while widow's
    chauffeur-driven
In sportscars pop from soda to lingerie shop,
    next the Station to Heaven
I will be pleased to show you the long-hand holograph at
    your request

LANDIS GORES
March 20, 1952

TURRET TOP TEMPEST

It seems to me that there is a tempest in a turret top-
Or is that what you call the new covers of a
        man's abode?
Because the modern architect wants to be
        modern and eat, too
It is not the Johnson and the Gores and the
        Breuers
That louse up the countryside we call
        our own New Canaan
But the people who have just got
        to be up with the
        Joneses (or is it the Johnsons?)
        have their new abode
Vaguely resemble what the poor
        designer originally had in mind
What with a playroom here, instead
        of there and perhaps a
Sunken tub to south instead of north
        it is all very
Discouraging to the artiste in soul (sic)
        as you can see
Super-markets rise where starry
        pure beauty ought
To be. Or not to be…that is the rankler of a
        Johnson's
Soul for, where he sits a house
        only tens yards further
From the tree which he assures me
        will make for perfect
Symmetry. I guess I might as well
        admit that I do not
Find perfect bliss in long blank walls
        and small round
Bumps, but who am I to these? My grandfather
Bought a place at Croton which has
        the style now featured

In those lovely creep-type
        Yorker cartoons. The
Ones where cobwebs brush the wings
        of bats and gentle,
Ghoul-like beings talk with modern
        wit. I suppose
That grandpa thought that he was
        rushing things a bit, but now
I secretly admit, I burned the place
        last spring.
So I say let these moderns be.
We'll have a new style soon,
You'll see. And live in islands hung
        in space
With shapes the like of which you
        find in Silvermine's
World famous school of art, Hold
        tight my little
Brethren. You ain't seen nothin' yet.

STONE-WALLED WHITMAN
March 20, 1952

O TEMPORA! O GORES!

Glass House Phil says Gores likes
    the overlapping plane
Judged by his prose we fear that he
    has overlapped again
If sixty five word sentences are the
    newest of the new,
We'll take Mansard roofs and cupolas,
    a widow's walk or two,
If "Decalogue" has come to mean,
    a ten-line bit of verse
Instead of the Ten Commandments
    we are ready for the hearse
If dear old Landis can but hand
    a non-handwritten holograph
We'll pay his way to Back Bay
    and throw in a free cenotaph.

CANTILEVER BEA
(The Petulant Skirt)
March 27, 1952

PIGEONS COO

Pigeons on the widows' walk
Chalking up their double talk
This is what they dovely cooed
Turtling in an antique mood

Johnson, Johansen, Gores and Noyes
    Other folks' woes to them are joys

Noyes and Johnson and Gores - Johansen:
    Come hell or high taxes, they all
    Keep their pants on.

Gores and Johansen, Noyes and Johnson
Revivalist houses they find no
    response in.

Johnson, Noyes, Johansen and Gores
Together they cry, "Nobis etempora
    nobis mores!"

EAVESDROPPER
March 27, 1952

"SO TEPEES ANY MORE"

(WITH APOLOGIES TO EDNA ST. VINCENT MILLAY)

Ogden! Don't you think you are
Just a wee bit insular–
Standing as you do, aghast
At the vista of the past
From the Station next to Heaven
Lightened with a little leaven?

So, I guess, the Indian, jeering
Watched the pale face in the clearing
Never use pole or pelt or
Other means of making shelter
Long approved by building code,
Raising up a new abode –

House no canny Indian would
Pass the door of if he could
"Ugh, this solid thing of horror?
(Perhaps a building of tomorrow)
"Lacks a red-skins prime utility
Lacks the squaws all portability.

Ogden, if you think upon't
Indian braves with painted bonnets
Never saunter now in Elm Street
Trading skins for things to eat
But those who took the "function" risk
Report that building yes, is brisk

Chatter, chatter, little teeth
How I wonder whose you beeth
Teeth like your ought not to bite
Or to overcome with fright
Those who build a tepee better
For the modern tepee-getter.

Teeth like yours, dear Ogden, really
In New Canaan sound quite silly
Let me voice a neighbors' thought
If in verse you must disport,
Before you pen your idle ventures
Sterilize your Knashing dentures

EDGAR A. KNIFFIN
March 27, 1952

TEPEE OR NOT TEPEE

Howdy! Kniffen, Edgar A.
Minstrel of the latest lay,
Architectural judge, impartial,
Sounder of the tecsin, martial
In behalf of modern tepees –
Inducers of the heeby-jeebies.

Pueblo built himself adobe
Houses of the Sixteenth Century–
Heap much like New Canaan "modern"
Roof much flat–cost many wampum.
Injun still walks streets of Taos
Much amused at modern chaos

Caused by Kniffs amusing view
That bureau drawers are something new;
That bebop should replace Beethoven,
Since bebop sells and Ludwig doesn't
Come, my little Princeton griffin,
Your logic's weak, your flat roofs leakin'

A CARPORT
April 3, 1952

AMEN
(WITH APOLOGIES TO THE READERS)

When Messrs. J. and J. and G. and N.
Are side by side with Christopher Wren
Editors historical
Will be satirical
About our Station Next to Heaven!

In publishing a town review,
Come twenty hundred and fifty-two,
Will anybody glorify
Or even try to justify
The building mode that caused this stew?

This Public Forum of so-called "verse"
Makes clear of late that many curse
In terms expostulate
How they abominate
What's happening to this universe.

ROCKIN' CHAIR ANNIE
April 3, 1952

MOSSES FROM AN OLD MANSARD

In architecture
There's conjecture

About that goddern
Bloomin' modern

Even so
We know

The man Baroque
Would likely choke,

If his castle so baronial
Were made over in Colonial;

And bulbous Jacobeans,
Themselves antiquarians,

Would soon question the origin
Of houses in the Georgian.

So hail to the flying buttresses and Ionic
But don't forget cantilevers and supersonic.

Acanthus, acanthus, Wren, Palladio;
Form follows function, from chair to radio

Chippendale cabriole Grindling, Gibbons;
Gropius, Van der Rohe, Robsjohn, Giggings

Morris Chair or African Camp
Guests will rest without a cramp –

Good things labeled "made today"
Don't toss the old away,

So why then let antiques
Call new things freaks?

Next time you prate the Heppelwhite
Don't forget that maybe Frank Lloyd's Wright

JUST ANON
April 3, 1952OH

OH TEMPERATURE! OH GORES!

Our modernists have turned to verse,
To speak of grave-stark trends and worse
In houses
Behold now down where Elm meets South
Their pudding – which in any mouth
Belouses.

Iambically, their lines don't scan,
Artistically, they mock the man,
These mouses.

Postlude
(danced to muted lutes)
Waltz me upon my widow's walk,
My mansard aged by pigeon'd chalk,
Unleash Victoria's best barrages
Upon the set without garages

NEW CANAAN FEDERATED WIGWAMISTS
April 3, 1952

169

LAMENT OF A MODERN

As a member of the modern generation,
    I would like to express my
consternation.
    On points modern and traditional,
Herewith; an argument controversial.

I'd rather not have to read Faust
and prefer Shostakovich to Strauss
Oh, Ruben's passé – I like Dali;
    and Johnny Ray tops Rudy Vallee.
E.E. Cummings and Eliot give me
a lift;
I never liked Bacon or Shakespeare
    or Swift.
Tho' great Pavolova once had her day;
    I think Martha Grahm's here to stay.
We're ahead of deVinci in things
    scientific;
In the age of atomics we've become
    quite prolific.
In matters of song Rogers and Hammerstein
    came to bat;
Dear Gilbert and Sullivan are
    very old hat;
And we've conquered the stage with
    our Lindsays Crouses
But we've failed most completely in
    building our houses!
Give me the Gothic, or even Rococo;
Mr. Johnson, I think you're just plain
    loco.
The vine covered cottage is one of
    my joys;
I can't sympathize with his friend,
    Mr. Noyes.
I'm modern, believe me, in all the
    new fads.
But these architects are the worst
    kind of cads.
I strive with this plea for some
    sublimation,
With heartfelt sincerity for my
    generation.

A MODERN MISS
April 10, 1952

IT TAKES A HEAP OF LIVING

It takes a heap of livin in a
    place to make it home
And I wish those guys like Johnson
    would take their plans and roam.
They're lousing up the countryside
    with buildings most alarming,
It isn't like New Canaan, where
    everythings been charming.
If Kniffen builds like Johnson and
    Johnson builds like Noyes,
Why don't they get some wooden
    blocks and play with them like
    toys.
Maybe I'm old fashioned or maybe
    I'm not keen
But when I take my monthly bath
    I'd rather not be seen.
So just to strike a sober note to end
    this little poem
It takes a heap o' living in a place
    to make it home.

EDGAR GUESS WHO?
April 17, 1952

CREDITS

NOTE: UNLESS OTHERWISE CREDITED, MARCEL BREUER QUOTES ARE FROM *MARCEL BREUER: BUILDINGS AND PROJECTS 1921–1961* (NEW YORK: FREDERICK A. PRAEGER, 1962).

58 Kniffen house: © Wayne Andrews/Esto
    Quote: Marcel Breuer lecture "On Architecture and
    Material," 1936

59 Kniffen house plan: William Earls

60 Johansen house: © Wayne Andrews/Esto

61 Johansen portrait courtesy John Johansen
    Clippings: McCalls magazine, June 1952

62 John Johansen rendering courtesy Avery Library,
    Columbia University
    Quote: *McCalls* Magazine

63 Quote: nterview in Stanfordville, New York, May 1999

64 Mills house: © Wayne Andrews/Esto
    Quote: Marcel Breuer lecture "Notes on Lectures1936–1948"

65 Quote: Marcel Breuer lecture "Sun and Shadow"
    Mills plan: William Earls

66 John Johansen rendering courtesy Avery Library,
    Columbia University
    Quote: interview in Stanfordville, New York, May 1999

67 Quote: interview in Stanfordville, New York, May 1999
    Dunham plan courtesy Christian Bjone

68 John Johansen rendering courtesy Avery Library,
    Columbia University
    Quote: interview in Stanfordville, New York, May 1999

69 Spray-form house: E. J. Cyr
    Quote: interview in Stanfordville, New York, May 1999

70 Hodgson house interior: © Ezra Stoller/Esto
    Hodgson house from street: William Earls
    Quote: Architectural Record, March 1953

71 Hodgson chimney: © Ezra Stoller/Esto
    Hodgson plan courtesy Philip Johnson/Alan Ritchie

72 Stackpole house east: William Earls
    Stackpole house southwest: William Earls

73 Stackpole plans: William Earls

74 Bremer house: Nina Bremer
    Quote: House & Home magazine, January 1953

75 Bremer plans courtesy Christian Bjone

76 Breuer on porch: Nina Bremer

77 Bremer stair: Ben Schnall

78 Breuer 2 house entry: E. J. Cyr
    Poem: Marcel Breuer lecture "Individual Expression
    Versus Order," 1961
    Quote: Marcel Breuer lecture "On Art Education," 1948

79 Breuer 2 house from street: E. J. Cyr
    Breuer 2 plan: William Earls
    Quote: Marcel Breuer lecture "Individual Expression
    Versus Order," 1961

80 Lee house rear: John Black Lee
    Quote: interview in New Canaan, Connecticut, June 2002

81 Lee plan courtesy John Black Lee

82 Lee house approach: William Earls

83 Lee house side: John Black Lee

84 Lee house porch: John Black Lee

85 Lee house office: John Black Lee

86 Lee house living room: John Black Lee

87 Lee house bedroom: John Black Lee

88 Riley house: William Earls

89 Riley plans: Chauncey Riley

90 Riley house west: William Earls

91 Riley house nook: William Earls

92 Riley house living room: © Ezra Stoller/Esto

93 Riley stairs: © Ezra Stoller/Esto

94 Irwin house from street: E. J. Cyr

95 Irwin house back courtesy The New Canaan Historical Society
    Quote: Holiday magazine, August 1952

96 Campbell house original: Ben Schnall

97 Campbell plan with additions courtesy Alan Goldberg

98 Campbell house painted: Allan Mitchell
    Quote: interview in New Canaan, Connecticut, March 2005
    Goldberg house under renovation: Allan Mitchell

99 Goldberg house: Allan Mitchell
    Goldberg with children: Allan Mitchell
    Quote: interview in New Canaan, Connecticut, March 2005

100 Goldberg house rear: William Earls

101 Goldberg house interior: Alan Goldberg

102 Ball house front: © Ezra Stoller/Esto
    Ball house northwest corner courtesy The New Canaan
    Historical Society
    Quote: House & Home magazine, January 1953

103 Ball house plan: courtesy Philip Johnson/Alan Ritchie

104 Goode house side: E. J. Cyr
    Quote: interview in Stanfordville, New York, May 1999

105 John Johansen rendering courtesy Avery Library,
    Columbia University
    Goode house corner: Sellwood
    Quote: interview in Stanfordville, New York, May 1999

106 Wiley house: © Ezra Stoller/Esto
    Quote courtesy Philip Johnson/Alan Ritchie

107   Wiley plans courtesy Philip Johnson/Alan Ritchie

108   Wiley house interior: © Ezra Stoller/Esto

109   Wiley house with barn: William Earls
       Quote: House & Home magazine, January 1953

110   Dickenson house: E. J. Cyr

111   Quote: House & Home magazine, January 1953
       Dickenson house demolition: William Earls

112   Noyes 2 house courtyard: © Ezra Stoller/Esto

113   Noyes 2 plan: courtesy Christian Bjone

114   Noyes 2 bedroom side: © Ezra Stoller/Esto
       Noyes 2 house from street: © Ezra Stoller/Esto
       Quote: Architectural Record, January, 1966

115   Noyes 2 living room: © Ezra Stoller/Esto

116   Rayford house approach: Pedro E. Guerrero

117   Rayford plan: William Earls

118   Rayford living room © Peter Aaron/ Esto

119   Rayford terrace: Pedro E. Guerrero
       Quote courtesy Pamela Gores

120   Rayford house front: David Verespy

121   Rayford house rear: David Verespy

122   Lee 2 house: Lisanti

123   Porch after renovation: William Earls
       Lee 2 plan: William Earls

124   Lee 2 entry: Joseph W. Molitor

125   Lee 2 clerestory: Joseph W. Molitor

126   Lee 2 kitchen: Studio New York Times

127   Mr. Mrs. Lee in kitchen: Lisanti

128   Warner house side: Robert Damora

129   Warner plan: courtesy Christian Bjone

130   Warner interior: Robert Damora

131   Warner from river: William Earls
       Quote: from The Second Treasury of Contemporary Houses
       (Architectural Record magazine)

132   Boissonas house back: © Ezra Stoller/Esto
       Boissonas house front: Pedro E. Guerrero

133   Boissonas plan courtesy Philip Johnson/Alan Ritchie

134   Boissonas pergola: William Earls
       Quote courtesy Philip Johnson/Alan Ritchie

135   Boissonas house rear: William Earls

136   Smallen house with front door: © Ezra Stoller/Esto

137   Smallen house side: © Ezra Stoller/Esto
       Clipping courtesy The New Canaan Advertiser

138   Mills house patio: Joseph W. Molitor

139   Mills plans: William Earls
       Quote: The Second Treasury of Contemporary Houses
       (Architectural Record magazine)
       Mills house front: E. J. Cyr

140   Mills triple-hung window: Marc Heldens

141   Mills living room: Marc Heldens

142   Celanese house front: Pedro E. Guerrero
       Celanese house rear: Pedro E. Guerrero

143   Celanese dining room: Pedro E. Guerrero
       Celanese living room: Pedro E. Guerrero

144   Irwin pool house corner: Robert Damora

145   Irwin pool house interior: Robert Damora
       Irwin pool house fireplace: Robert Damora
       Irwin pool house plan: William Earls
       Quote courtesy Pamela Gores

146   Teaze house courtesy Lillian Wolfe

147   Teaze plan: William Earls

148   McCarthy house: Alan Goldfinger

149   McCarthy kitchen: Alan Goldfinger
       McCarthy plan: William Earls

150   DeSilver house bridge: Lisanti

151   DeSilver plans: William Earls

152   DeSilver house construction: Syd Greenberg

153   DeSilver house tour: Syd Greenberg

154   Parsons living room: © Ezra Stoller/Esto

155   Clippings: New York Times Magazine, July 25, 1965

156   Day house retaining wall: Pedro E. Guerrero

157   Day plans: William Earls

158   Day house night: Allan Mitchell

159   Day house approach: Pedro E. Guerrero
       Day house courtyard: Pedro E. Guerrero

160   Luthold house rear: Pedro E. Guerrero

161   Luthold plan: William Earls

162   Luthold roof edges: William Earls

163   Luthold exteriors: William Earls

ACKNOWLEDGMENTS

In some ways, it took the entire town of New Canaan to write this book. However, specific individuals need to be recognized for their contributions:

Special thanks to my sister Molly

Thank you to Janet Lindstrom and Sharon Turo of The New Canaan Historical Society

I thank these individuals for their contributions:

Christian Bjone
Robert and Sirkka Damora
Laurent T. DuPont
Jean Cauthorne Ely
Alan Goldberg
Pamela Gores
John Black Lee
Hilary Lewis
John Johansen
Philip Johnson and the office of Philip Johnson/Alan Ritchie
Monika Mittal
Lillian Wolfe

I thank the following periodicals:

Architectural Record
New Canaan Advertiser
New York Times Magazine

And, finally, thank you to the photographers:

John Bukovcik
Nina Bremer
E. J. Cyr
Robert Damora
ESTO Photographics
Syd Greenberg
Alan Goldfinger
Pedro Guerrero
Marc Heldens
Hester + Hardaway
Allan Mitchell
Joseph Molitor
Ben Schnall
David Verespy